# THE NURSERY YEARS

A climbing frame is a great help to the growth of little children. It can be made to any size by a ladder-maker. If stably fixed, it is a very safe plaything; and as most children of three to seven years hardly ever tire of it, and can use it in " playing houses " as well as for climbing, it is a very good investment.

# THE
# NURSERY YEARS

*The Mind of the Child*
*from Birth to Six Years*

## SUSAN ISAACS

*Introduction by Millie Almy*

SCHOCKEN BOOKS • NEW YORK

# CONTENTS

# INTRODUCTION TO THE 1968 EDITION

THE present edition of *The Nursery Years* marks the thirtieth anniversary of the first American edition. The book was first published in England in 1929. It reappears at a time when the "facts" of child development, on which Dr. Isaacs placed great stress, are expanding at a great rate, are understood to represent greater complexity, and are subject to continual revision as the nature of development is better understood. The handful of nursery schools she cites has grown into a great number of programs for young children. Variously labelled as prekindergartens, "Head Start," or child development centers—as well as nursery schools—they have spread through all segments of the population and currently attract much attention.

Looking back over the forty years that have brought this to pass, one is tempted to label them the years of discovery and rediscovery of the young child, and of various aspects of his development. Just as the first edition of *The Nursery Years* contributed to the initial discovery, so this edition seems destined to contribute to the rediscovery.

When *The Nursery Years* was first published, the scientific study of young children in the United States, often in newly established nursery schools, was well under way in a number of universities. The 1930 White

House Conference on children hailed the twentieth century as the century of the child. It stressed the importance of the "whole" child and the interrelatedness of his physical, mental, emotional, and social development.

It was in this context that the first American edition of *The Nursery Years* appeared and was awarded the 1937 "Outstanding Book of the Year" medal by *Parents Magazine*. A committee of leaders in parent education and child study cited the admirable clarity of its explanation of the principles of child guidance, based on the established facts of physical and mental growth. They also were impressed with the way Dr. Isaacs dealt with the subtler aspects of child development.

*The Nursery Years,* in contrast to the prescriptions for habit training that had characterized much of the literature of the time, is concerned with the child's point of view, as well as that of the adult. It gives clues to understanding his fears, his hostilities, and his jealousy. It suggests how his play simultaneously reveals his concerns and serves as a medium for his learning and knowing. It is significant that at least one edition of *The Nursery Years* bore the subtitle "The Mind of the Child from Birth to Six Years."

Nineteen thirty-seven was a depression year. During the depression, and in the years of World War II, WPA nursery schools and Lanham Act day-care centers provided opportunities for the study of more representative groups of American children than had previously been possible. But these were also years when few funds were available for research. After the war, many middle-class children went to nursery schools; some were private or cooperative, some clearly commercial. Some children also participated in nursery school programs in day-care centers. But there was no great push to expand facilities, and interest in child development research continued at a low ebb.

In 1950 the White House Conference attempted to consolidate what was then known about personality development. Drawing on the work of Erikson, it emphasized the special contribution of infancy and the pre-school years to later development. Trust, worthy selfhood, initiative—these were the watchwords for the nursery years, while mastery was highlighted in the elementary-school years. The scheme set forth implied the constant interplay between the child's emotional concerns and his developing understanding of his world. In the language of today, cognition and affective development were seen as intertwined.

By this time psychoanalytic theories had either directly or indirectly dominated child development research and had permeated the child-rearing advice of many experts. Such popularization often leads to distortion and, looking back, this appears to have been the case in the 1950's. Too often, the free expression of impulse rather than its eventual mastery and direction was made to seem to be the primary goal for the nursery years.

Current critics of this trend paint a picture that is probably blacker than reality. Nevertheless, it is true that, for a time, in some nursery schools and kindergartens, one sought vainly for evidence that teachers, however concerned they might be with the children's emotional and social development, had any notion of their intellectual power. Susan Isaacs, with her belief that the intelligence and power of observation of young children are generally underestimated, could only have been appalled at the intellectual sterility of some of these programs.

Likewise, one suspects she would never have regarded as sufficient any counsel to parents based only on a consideration of the emotional hazards to a child's development. Parents have an obligation, as she makes clear in this volume, to provide appropriate intellectual stimulation for the precocious and the backward, as well as the more ordinary, child.

Her point of view, if not actually played down during the 1950's, was certainly not emphasized. By the 1960's, however, the intellectual aspects of the young child's development were, in a sense, rediscovered, and stimulation for the young child is now deemed so important that government is beginning to step in to supplement what parents can do.

This rediscovery of early childhood, and particularly of its strategic role in later intellectual development, dates perhaps from 1957, when Sputnik highlighted some of the inadequacies of American public education —particularly in mathematics and science. Faced with the problem of constructing new curricula, educators and specialists in the disciplines turned to psychology and to child development research for information on the ways children learn to conceptualize. They found a paucity of research relating to cognitive development in the American literature. However, they rediscovered the research of Jean Piaget, the Swiss contemporary of Susan Isaacs.

Piaget had begun his studies of children's thinking in the early 1920's. Although translated into English and briefly cited in most child psychology texts, these early works were rather neglected in this country. Susan Isaacs, who was from 1924 to 1927 principal of the Malting House School in Cambridge, was greatly stimulated by Piaget's work. Her book *Intellectual Growth in Young Children*, first published in 1930, reflects her interest, and can almost be regarded as a running debate with him. She found in her observations of children playing and working together evidence of thought of a different caliber from that which children revealed to Piaget when he interviewed them.

In turn, some of Piaget's later work (of which there is a great deal) shows his awareness of Susan Isaacs' criticisms and some modification of certain of his techniques in the light of it. However, with the exception of the volume *Play, Dreams and Imitation*, Piaget is not as concerned with the personal aspects of the child's understanding or with the way affect permeates his cognition as was Susan Isaacs. His studies reveal the cognitive behavior that is typical of children of different ages. They delineate the steps by which children move from egocentric, perceptually dominated intuitions, to more systematic, logical, and truly conceptual thought Focused on concepts basic to mathematics and science, much of his research has been immediately useful to American psychologists interested in improving intellectual functioning.

One such psychologist is Jerome Bruner, whose book *The Process of Education*, published in 1960, has been influential in curriculum reforms in kindergarten and the early grades and has also highlighted the importance of earlier childhood education. In this volume Bruner draws on Piaget to show that the same concept may be very differently apprehended by children of different ages.

He also makes the optimistic and much quoted statement that any concept can be taught in some intellectually
honest way to a child of any age. Those who have tried
such teaching have not always found it as simple as
Bruner's quotation, taken out of context, might imply.
One suspects that the successful teacher is precisely the
one who has enough of Susan Isaacs' sensitivity to the
inner life of the child to know how to approach him and
when to teach him.

Another psychologist whose work derives from Piaget
is J. McVicker Hunt. His *Intelligence and Experience,*
published in 1961, reviews some of the earlier research
on the role of nature and nurture, training and matura-
tion in intellectual development and comes to the conclusion that it should be possible to "govern the child's
encounter with his environment in such a way as to increase his intellectual development." The clue to an effective governing, he believes, lies in providing a good
"match" between the child's current level of understanding and the new experience. Montessori's materials are
cited as an example of such a match.

In a sense, Susan Isaacs in *The Nursery Years,* and
more specifically in *Intellectual Growth in Young Children,* is also interested in matching new experience to
present understanding. But she evidently had even more
faith in the child's ability to learn in his own way,
through imposing his own order on his materials, than
did Montessori.

The Bruner and the Hunt volumes marked the beginning of a spate of cognitive research. On the one hand,
work, not only with the three-, four-, and five-year-olds
but also with infants and two-year-olds, has increased
steadily throughout the 1960's. Much of it is purely

experimental. Under laboratory conditions, the extent of the young child's learning, his ability to grasp fairly complex ideas if they can be broken into simple components, has been surprisingly good. On the other hand, apparent gains are sometimes not sustained over long periods of time or under differing conditions.

In the classroom the effectiveness of cognitive intervention has also varied. There have been, for example, some instances of successful attempts to raise the I.Q.'s of disadvantaged children, but perhaps more instances of failure. Earlier beginnings, more intensive work with both children and parents, more alertness to individual ways of learning and thinking, and continued follow-up appear to be in order.

The needs of the disadvantaged are so great that almost any kind of intervention may seem better than none. All the evidence so far suggests that the most effective intervention provides direct and systematic intellectual stimulation. But there is little to suggest that the child, be he disadvantaged or privileged, who is challenged intellectually is necessarily less prone to emotional concern, less aware of fatigue, hunger, or of his desire for physical activity and social response than is the child who lacks cognitive stimulation.

The "whole child" cliché of the 1930's is perhaps due for rediscovery. We can as easily make the mistake of emphasizing the intellectual at the expense of physical, emotional, and social, as the 1950's made of overemphasizing the emotional.

At such a time the wisdom of *The Nursery Years* becomes especially meaningful.

Susan Isaacs was a scientist. Trained in psychology, in logic, and in psychoanalysis, she was, according to those who knew her, ever alert to new sources of knowledge. Her interest in securing empirical evidence to support or, if need be, to refute theory is clearly apparent in the careful observations she made of the Malting House children and reported in *Intellectual Growth in Young Children* and the companion volume, *Social Development in Young Children.*

From these, and from her comments in *The Nursery Years,* one may surmise what some of her reactions would be to recent research and experimentation in this country were she living today. The newer studies of young children, and particularly of their cognitive functioning, would be of great interest to her. But just as she cautions parents in *The Nursery Years* against taking the norms of child development as absolute, and urges them to study their own children, so she would insist on checking laboratory and experimental findings in more intensive and comprehensive studies in natural settings. Sensitive to the child's ways of experiencing, she would be concerned with the personal significance of his learning and whether or not it clarified his understanding or contributed to the confusions of his fantasy.

*The Nursery Years* encourages the parent to view himself as a participant in the inner life of the child, rather than a mere observer of his behavior. It is from such a stance that one begins not only to understand his thinking, but also how to plan the routines of his daily living in ways to avoid needless frustration. To understand in this way is not to try to interpret the child to himself, nor is it to meddle in the fantasy of his play. Rather it is to attend to what he reveals of himself and the world as he experiences them, and it is to temper one's expectations accordingly.

The reader who comes to *The Nursery Years* for the first time may wonder to what extent the knowledge of child development on which it was based is still valid. There are a number of places where the emphasis might be somewhat different were the book to be written today. Today's parents, for example, are much less restrictive about sexual matters than they were forty years ago. Whether or not this shift has changed the character of the young child's conflicts is, of course, debatable.

Again, Dr. Isaacs' statement that intelligence is mainly a function of heredity rather than of environment fails to do justice to the complexity of the interaction among genetic and environmental factors as they are now understood. From a more practical view, however, her recommendations for the nurture of individual intelligence read almost as though she had been familiar with some of the more recent theory and research.

All in all, this little volume, so clearly written, so free from the psychological jargon that besets both scientific and popular writing today, stands ready to lead parents, teachers, and possibly researchers toward discovery, or rediscovery, of the young child. He is cognitive, but not merely so; emotional, but not completely so. He has mind, but he also has muscles. He is indeed a whole child—a person.

MILLIE ALMY

January, 1968

# THE NURSERY YEARS

# CHAPTER I

## WHAT SHOULD WE DO?

**THE need for knowledge.** Not so very long ago it was taken for granted that parents had by nature or tradition most of the knowledge needed to enable them to bring up their children well. The baby then wore swaddling clothes so that he should not kick, and a tight belt so that he could not breathe. He was kept carefully away from " draughts " and fresh air, and heavily clothed so that he should not catch cold. He was fed when he cried, and given soothing syrup or a none-too-clean comforter when he could not be fed.

Now, however, we leave the infant free to kick and breathe ; we not only put him to sleep with wide-open windows or out in the garden, but we let him lie and roll naked to the very sun and air from which we used to shelter him so carefully. So far from trusting the mere affection and natural knowledge of the nursing mother, we feed him by the clock, at three- or four-hour intervals. When his stomach is thus respected, and his need for light and air and free movement and quiet rest is met, he has a far greater chance than formerly of living through his first year, of escaping infantile diarrhœa and rickets and the other ills of babyhood, and of growing steadily and sturdily throughout his childhood. And he is altogether a healthier and a happier baby than he used to be.

The important thing about this change in our belief as to what is best for children's bodies is that it is not simply a change of custom, nor the passing of one tradition in favour of another. It is that mothers and nurses have begun to turn away from mere custom and blind tradition, to science. Hearsay and habit are now no longer enough. Many practices that had been taken for granted for centuries have been found to be false guides when carefully tested; and we have now begun to base baby-rearing on proved scientific knowledge about food and sleep and clothing, the effects of light and air, and ways of preventing disease.

In the care of the child's mind also, this is beginning to be true; but it is not yet by any means as true as it might be. We still tend largely to take it as a matter of course that we know by nature, or by the experience of our training in childhood, what is best for our children's mental health; and whenever the child behaves in a way that does not please us, we are ready to act. We do so, out of our own good or bad humour at the moment, out of a habit of acting so, out of our " principles "; but rarely out of a full knowledge of what in the child's mind has led him to do the thing we don't like. Yet without that knowledge, we cannot be sure that we are dealing with him in the way most likely to help him. Without it, we move in the dark, and may do much harm, with the best intentions in the world. Children need all our affection and sympathy; but they need also all our intelligence, and our patient and serious efforts to understand the ways of their mental growth. And we cannot leave this to their professional teachers, for they come upon the scene of the child's life too late in the day. By the time children go to school, some of the most important things that ever happen to them are already in the past. It is not too much to say, in the light of recent psychological studies, that the main lines of their behaviour are by then firmly fixed.

**Difficulties.** Perhaps we can most readily gain a lively sense of our need for knowledge if we look at some of the typical situations happening from day to day between parents and children.

Let us take first some of the admitted problems, about which even the least reflective parent must feel perplexity from time to time. The question of children's lying, for instance. A child denies having done something we know he has done ; what is the best way of dealing with this ? Ought we to " punish " him severely, or talk to him about the wickedness of lying ? Will he go on lying if we don't ? What makes him lie ? And the younger child who may be heard telling " stories " to his playmates about wonderful things he has done, or about his possessions at home—he also is " lying ". Ought we to treat this in the same way ?

What should we reply when John and Mary ask embarrassing questions as to " where babies come from " ? Is it best to evade, or lie about black bags or the gooseberry bush ? Or to give a simple and frank answer, as far as we know how to do so ? And will such an answer content them, and lead them to think no more about it ?

A child of three or four will sometimes bite his playmates or his mother, either in playful affection or in temper. Most mothers are shocked and worried by this, and it may be a serious difficulty in his play with others. What leads him to bite ? Is it abnormal ? And what should we do about it ?

Again, when we find our small boy playing with his genital organ in bed, or when sitting dreamily in the daytime—what should we say or do ? Will a scolding or whipping stop the habit ? How has it arisen ? Is it always the result of suggestion from some playmate, or can it occur spontaneously ? Will it go on if we don't do anything about it ?

Or how shall we deal with those irrational but overwhelming fears which little children sometimes suddenly develop—e.g., a paroxysmal terror of being put into the bath or of having their heads washed, a great fear of a conjuring show which other children love, or such excessive anxiety about ordinary small bumps or abrasions as to cause vomiting ?

**Everyday problems.** It is not, however, only about such obviously difficult situations that we can ask " Why ? " and " How ? " There are few happenings between us and our children which are not open to scrutiny, when once we cease to take for granted the child's needs and the rightness of our own first impulses. The infant of about a year, for instance, finds pleasure in throwing his spoon or doll down to the floor over and over again, for mother or nurse to pick up. The latter tire of the game long before he does, and may end up by telling him " not to be naughty ". Why does he do it ? Has it any value for his development ? Is it mere " mischievousness ", needing correction ?

A child of, say, four years, left to play in the garden,

will climb about on the railings, tearing his clothes and making his knees dirty. Should we scold him for this? Again, is it mere perversity and thoughtlessness, or some impulse of growth towards poise and skill?

A little girl of three years is alone in the drawing-room. Her mother in the next room presently hears a quiet voice saying : " Up-down-atross, up-down-atross "; and on going in, finds her daughter chalking the letter A, which she has just learnt, all over the walls. What should she say? " Don't do that ever again, you naughty child ! "? Or " would you mind writing on your own blackboard, not the walls ? "? Does the child do it because she wants to mess the walls, or because she is eager to write like the grown-ups and so turns to the thing nearest to hand?

Another child of five years has such a passion for keeping his hands and clothes clean that when he is given some clay to model with, he does not want to use it, " because it makes my hands dirty ". Has his mother reason to be pleased about this? Is it a sign of healthy development?

A little girl of twenty months wants passionately to be allowed to feed herself, although she can't manage it without spilling. When her nurse insists on feeding her, or at least holding her hand while she tries to do it, the child flies into a furious rage and won't eat. Is this just naughtiness? Should she be made to obey and submit docilely to being fed?

Children of all ages are attracted by fire and matches. Most parents are very nervous of this until the children are eight or nine years of age, or more; yet the boy of four or five will play with matches whenever he can get hold of them. May this not mean something for his growth in knowledge and skill ?   Ought we for safety's sake to forbid him to touch them—or can we perhaps find some way of letting him learn early to handle them safely ?

And when a child says " I shan't ", climbs on the drawing-room chairs with dirty boots, or leaves the taps running in the bathroom ;  when another child pinches her younger sister, or refuses to eat what is put before her ;  when either of them is found stealing sugar from the pantry, or has " an accident "—in any of these emergencies, is it quite clear and certain that we know at once what is the wisest thing to do ?

**What should we do ?**   Obviously, we can only decide what we " ought " to do and what we " should " say when we understand what the children's behaviour means to them, and know the actual effect on them of what we do.

We cannot, of course, carry these queries about with us in daily practice.   Faced with the situations, we have not time to ask ourselves such questions, nor would it be any help if we were always weighed down by a too-present sense of responsibility.   Sometimes it *would* be better to postpone any action until we had taken time for thought—since a little reflection is worth a lot of interference ;  but on the whole, it is clearly best to do our thinking and questioning away from the children, so that our relation with them can be easy and direct ; and to do it beforehand, so that our wisdom may have time to get into our habits.

I have begun by raising some of the everyday practical problems of the everyday parent ;  and as far as the limits of space allow, I will try to answer them.   But I shall do this simply to illustrate broad guiding principles, and not as cut-and-dried practical advice. I cannot offer the latter, because parents differ, children differ, and circumstances differ. What may be good advice for one may be unsound for another. It is, indeed, an essential part of intelligent parenthood to break away from rules of thumb, and learn to judge each situation for each child on its own merits in the light of a general understanding of the ways of growth.

What helps most in the long run is the ability to enter into the child's own world with an informed sympathy, the general sense that his problems are problems of growth, and a patient and friendly interest in the ways of that growth.

CHAPTER II

## PLAY AND GROWTH

**T**HE **human infant and others.** Setting aside for a time, then, our practical problems, let us look at children from the broad general point of view of human biological history.

If we compare human infants with the young of other animals, we see, in the first place, that the human babe is far more helpless and more closely dependent upon parental care than any other animal young, and that the period of childhood lasts much longer. Secondly, the human child has a far greater capacity for learning than any other young animal. Mammals as a whole are far more able to learn by individual experience than, say, the insects, the reptiles, or even the birds, who all live by relatively fixed instincts. And even among the mammals, some are more teachable than others. It can be said in general that the more helpless and dependent upon the parents' care the young of an animal species are, and the longer the time this care is needed, the more intelligent and adaptable the individual members of the species are found to be, and the less do they live by fixed and inherited ways of behaviour. And of man, above all animals, these things are true. The greater length of his childhood and the greater need of his young for protection and care are closely

8

bound up with his far fewer fixed and inborn modes of action, and his immensely greater ability to profit (and to lose) by individual experience. This is the biological meaning of his childhood, and the basis of his civilisation.

**The playing animals.** If now we compare again the more adaptable and intelligent animals with the less, for instance, the reptiles and fishes with the mammals, we notice something which throws much light on human childhood—viz.: the fact that the animals which are able to *learn* more are also able to *play* more. Those with fixed and inherited instincts play not at all; the young behave as the old from the beginning, and there is nothing to add to the wisdom of the species. But the playing animals, and in proportion as they play, gain something of an individual wisdom. They are the curious, the experimental animals. The young lamb skips, but only for a short time, and soon settles down into sheep-like stolidity. Whereas the kitten plays on, and tries its way about the world with playful paw and nose, long after its size and age might lead us to expect a sober maturity. Those animals nearest of all to ourselves, the monkey and the ape, are like us in keeping the will to play even into maturity; but no animal young play so freely, so inventively, so continually and so long as human children.

All this would suggest that play means much as a way of development for the learning animal; and those who have watched the play of children have long looked upon it as Nature's means of individual education. Play is indeed the child's work, and the means whereby he grows and develops. Active play can be looked upon as a sign of mental health; and its absence, either of some inborn defect, or of mental illness.

**The meaning of play.** To get the fullest light on what play actually means to the child, we must think of it in relation to his immediate present, and his need to adapt to the world around him day by day. We find children of different ages at play doing things which will lead to an increase of skill or power or understanding. The infant of about one year joyfully practises over and over the sounds which will presently become words, and the words he is just learning to use. The older child's pleasure is to climb, jump, run, skip, throw a ball, and repeat endlessly the movements which will develop strength and agility of legs and arms and fingers.

Through play also, he adds to his knowledge of the world. The healthy happy child is constantly exploring everything around him—first of all with his mouth ; then, later, with active touch. He pulls things to pieces, and pokes about to see what is inside. He turns the taps, and pulls the books out from the shelves, and throws his doll on the fire to see whether it will burn. No experimental scientist has a greater thirst for new facts than an ordinary healthy active child.

Not all his play, however, is directed to exploring the physical world or practising new skills. Much of it is social in direction, and belongs to the world of phantasy. He plays at being father and mother, the new baby sister, the policeman, the soldier ; at going for a journey, at going to bed and getting up, and all the things which he sees grown-ups doing. Here also his play makes it easier for him to fit himself into his social world. When he becomes the father and the mother, he wins an imaginative insight into their attitude to him, and some little understanding of their sayings and doings ; and momentarily feels their powers and great gifts (as they seem to him) as his own. All the things he may not do and cannot be in real life, he is able to do and be in this play world, which thus gives him a refuge from the moment-to-moment pressure of real demands, and lets him return to these refreshed.

**Play as education.** I shall say more of these profoundly important aspects of play later on. For the moment perhaps enough has been said to show how large a value children's play has for all sides of their growth. How great an ally the thoughtful parent can find it ! And how fatal to go against this great stream of healthy and active impulse in our children ! That " restlessness " and inability to sit still; that " mischievousness " and " looking inside " and eternal " Why ? " ; that indifference to soiled hands and torn clothes for the sake of running and climbing and digging and exploring—these are not unfortunate and accidental ways of childhood which are to be shed as soon as we can get rid of them. They are the glory of the human child, his human heritage. They are at once the representatives in him of human adventurousness and hard-won wisdom, and the means by which he in his turn will lay hold of knowledge and skill, and add to them.

**Some problems solved.** Already, perhaps, some of the questions put in the first chapter can be answered. We can see some meaning now in the pleasure the young child feels in throwing down his spoon, in the climbing of the older child, in the experiments with matches, in the writing on the walls. And we can see that, as educators, we have to deal with these impulses in such a way as to make the fullest use of their educational value for the child, without cutting across the reasonable interests of the adult in the family. Sometimes, of course, these latter are unreasonable, or fictitious. If we ourselves cannot be happy unless our children are sitting quite still and keeping spotlessly clean all the moments of the day, then it is we who need to be changed. If we will not give them anything to chalk on, either a board or piece of wall of their own, then surely it is we who are selfish and obstructive. But such stupidities aside, it can be agreed that the comfort and convenience of the grown-ups have a reasonable claim to consideration. How can we find ways of ensuring that these claims shall not work uneducatively for the children ? It is at least one step forward if we are honest in admitting that it *is* our own comfort and convenience which lead us so often to check the children's games—and if we cease to call it the children's " naughtiness ".

**The child and the man.** Let us look further at some of the general characters of childhood. If we compare the body of the infant, the child and the man, we see very clearly that the difference is not one of size only, but also of the proportions of the various parts. In the babe, the head is about twice the relative size of the man's whilst the legs are only three-fourths, and the arms much longer. Growth is thus not a simple increase in total size, but brings a varying increase of the different parts of the body. And this is itself by no means a chance affair, but is related to the needs of the body as a whole at each stage of development. The new-born babe, for example, cannot digest any food but milk ; his eyes and ears are not sufficiently developed to enable him to look after himself, and he is wholly dependent on his mother's arms for shelter, and her breast for nourishment. What he needs to do, he can do—cling to his mother and suck. His legs, therefore, do not need to be long (as those of a foal have to be) ; and they remain for some time folded up very much as they were in the womb. Along with these differences in outward form go certain physiological differences. The bones, for instance, are at first very soft. The gradual straightening out of the legs and first growth in relative length goes along not only with the gradual hardening of the bones, by which they become able to hold the body erect, but also with the development of sight and hearing and touch, and the general gain in muscular power and balance which makes walking possible about the end of the first year. At this time, too, the child begins to digest starchy foods, and so to gain a source of the much greater energy which he now needs for his freer and more vigorous movements.

These facts of physical growth and bodily needs are clear and easy to grasp. We don't imagine that the child is ill because he can't digest meat and bread at birth, nor think him abnormal because he can't hold a spoon or walk and talk. We don't think he *ought* to do these things, nor try to force the young infant to be like ourselves. We take him as he is, and try to meet his actual needs. In other words, we base our ideas of what is healthy and desirable upon the actual facts of normal development.

**Growth of mind.** If we come to the child's mind with the same direct observation, we find that the same general modes of difference, intimately bound up with the stages of bodily growth, hold there also. It is, however, more difficult for us to see this simply and clearly than in the case of bodily growth. We tend, on the whole, to err in two opposite directions ; to behave, to begin with, as if young infants had no mind at all, and only physical needs ; and then, when they reach three to five years of age, to assume that they are responsible moral beings like ourselves. We underestimate altogether, for instance, the powers of observation and readiness for impressions of the infant during, say, the second year of life, and the depth and intensity of his feelings towards his parents. Whereas with children old enough to talk and to listen, children who can, if we demand it, learn to seem outwardly polite and orderly and unselfish, we commonly over-estimate their ability to live easily up to our moral and personal standards, and to understand our adult customs.

Probably both mistakes are due to the illusion of speech. Because the infant is dumb, we assume that he has no mind ; because the toddler can use some of our words, we hardly doubt that he can be made to feel as we do. We don't realise that the general meaning of children's speech to them may be in many ways different from ours. Careful students of children's talk, however, have been able to show very clearly that this is so ; and that if we would know what the world is like to the young child while he is learning our language, we in our turn have to learn what he means by his. Children's speech is, of course, no less closely bound up with their feelings and wishes than with their judgment and reasoning ; and all these are in their turn intimately connected with their bodily growth. It is not simply that mental growth goes on at the same time as physical —it is that the two are most closely related to each other at every stage. The world must needs be a very different place to the infant at the breast from what it is to the free-running, question-asking child of four, or to the grown man. There is, of course, plenty of " human nature " in both children and men ; nevertheless, each has his own way of mental life, and his own special needs. And for our purposes it is perhaps more important to understand the differences than to stress the likenesses.

**The child's world.** It cannot, of course, be very easy for us to gain a clear idea of what the world is like to a very young child, just because it must be so different from our own. But by patient listening to the talk of even little children, and watching what they do, with the one purpose of understanding them, we can imaginatively feel their fears and angers, their bewilderments and triumphs ; we can wish their wishes, see their pictures and think their thoughts. When, as a small example, a boy of three wonderingly asks a friendly grown-up, " *Why* won't people do nothing if people don't say nothing ? " and on gentle questioning as to *what* " people don't say ", replies " when they don't say ' please ' "—we do get a sudden glimpse into the puzzlement which our rigid and arbitrary rules about manners may bring to little children.

With the infant, however, we have not even the help of halting speech. It needs a far closer and more patient study, and a far greater leap of the imagination, to bring us insight into the world of the wordless babe. Yet we must try to gain it, if we would know how his growth goes on, what his difficulties may be, and how to help him over them.

# CHAPTER III

## THE BEGINNINGS

I SHALL try in this chapter to enter into the mental life of the infant at birth, and during his first year of growth, by noticing in as much detail as possible what sort of things happen to him, what he can and cannot do, and what feelings and changes of feeling he shows.

**The mind of the infant.** It would be the greatest mistake to think that the baby needed nothing but bodily care in his first year, and that his mind only began to grow, say, when he began to talk. Even the quite young infant has very powerful wishes and feelings and phantasies. And these have all the stronger hold over him, just because his power of making them effective is as yet so feeble. Far more goes on behind those wide-open infant eyes than most people imagine. Knowledge is lacking, understanding has not yet begun ; but wants and wishes, fears and angers, love and hate are there from the beginning.

**Birth and before it.** At birth the babe has already had some limited experience. He has been held in a protecting fluid that would feel to him the same all over, and no light or changes of warmth and cold could come to him ; but it is likely that vibrations of various kinds would be carried to him, possibly even sounds ; and he has been able to move his limbs a little. As against the vast experience of birth itself, however, what happens before must be almost as nothing. Birth brings the sharpest, severest change of life. The babe is pushed and pulled, often under severe pressure, out of his still deep peace into the world of cold and moving air, light and sharp sound, and constant change. With his protesting movements, he draws the cold air into his lungs, and sends it out again with his first cry.

**The new-born.** The movements of the new-born are few and rather vague ; sucking movements with the lips and tongue, twitchings of the nostrils in breathing, more vigorous movements of the chest and throat in crying, twistings of the hand and curling of the fingers, turning of the head. The two eyes move independently of each other ; so do the fingers and toes. None of these movements is at first definite or controlled, although sucking quickly becomes so. And the baby as a whole is limp. The head flops, the limbs make no resistance to the way we move them or the position we put them in. There is one striking exception to this lack of tone— the firm grasp of the baby's hand on anything put within its palm.

Within a day or two he will, however, actually seek the breast, turning his mouth to it if it touch his cheek, or if it is near enough for him to smell the milk. As early as this he will turn his eyes to seek a light brought near him, although he cannot yet focus it ; and we can tell that his awareness of space is vague and confused, since he finds it difficult, for instance, to get his thumb into his mouth, and will for a long time reach out towards any bright object, reachable or not. Besides these directed movements, he sometimes moves spontaneously, waving his arms and legs about in vague, random ways.

**Movement and space.** Within the first month, great advances can be seen. The sucking movements are well established, and the eyes work together most of the time (although under the stress of fear they may turn apart even as late as the end of the year). There are plenty of spontaneous experimental movements of all parts of the body, and more general muscular tone.

The babe very quickly learns to focus his eyes on a bright object and to follow its movement, and the general education of his eyes and ears and active touch and muscular skill goes on apace. The early random movements of his arms and legs lead to definite physical experiences. He bangs his hand on the side of the cot, for instance, feels the sharp hard resistance and perhaps a little pain, turns his eyes and looks at what has met his hand, and so begins to draw together what the hand does and what the eye sees into his first notions of space. The near distances are grasped first—the sizes of things he can actually handle and reach. Only after he begins to walk does the child come to appreciate larger spaces. When a year old, he will still sometimes reach out for quite distant objects, and literally " cry for the moon ". And much has yet to be learnt even then about the appearances of common things. Even at a year and a half, the child may try to pick up a sunbeam off the floor, to take hold of his own image in a mirror, or to pull a trickle of water from a sponge as if it were a string. To us this seems strange, because the sight and the feel of these everyday things are so closely fused that they seem inseparable. But the child has to *learn* that a particular appearance always goes along with a certain sort of touch.

**Touch.** The feel of things is of course far more

fundamental for the child than their look. Even in the womb, the sense of touch is probably well developed; and after birth, touch is the first way of knowing things. The child responds to the touch of the nipple or the feel of sheltering arms long before he has learnt to *see* the breast or his mother's face. The most *real* things in those days, and perhaps throughout infancy and early childhood, must be *things that can be touched*. Probably their only rivals in the very beginning are things that can be tasted and smelled. Within the first day, the baby will turn away from a nipple smeared with petroleum, and when only two or three weeks old, he will refuse medicines with certain odours. Whereas he will turn *towards* the breast if he is held near enough to smell the milk, without touching it. The comforting odours of the breast and body must make up quite a large part of the babe's actual experience of his mother.

For the young infant, it comes as a thrilling discovery that things which can't be touched but only seen are nevertheless really " there ". And after that, much later, the child comes to realise that things may be effectively " there " although they can neither be seen nor touched. This is the source of the delight in the game of " peek-a-bo ", when the loved face of mother or father disappears behind a curtain or handkerchief, and the child waits breathlessly for its reappearance, and shouts with glee when it comes. If we do this with a child of nine months, we can often see a strained look of anxiety on his face while he waits for renewed sight of the loved person—as if he were afraid that they would never come back, or had ceased to be " there " because he couldn't see them. The more experienced one-year-old shows more confidence that they will reappear ; he has come to " know " that they are still there although he can't see them.

**Hearing.** Hearing is the least developed of the senses at birth. The first responses are only to sudden violent noises, which shock the child into twitching the face and body and even screaming. But from the sixth week onwards, varying with the child, milder sounds begin to awake attention, and he will turn his head to listen. After this, hearing develops rapidly, and the babe will soon come to know the everyday sounds of his tending and bathing, and the voice of mother or nurse. Between the second and fourth months, most children become very sensitive to different tones of voice, and may be profoundly affected by them. It may make a great difference to his nervous health whether he is surrounded by soft encouraging voices and quiet steps, or by harsh and shrill tones, frequent scoldings and banging of doors.

**Skill.** By the time he is four months old, the baby can be felt definitely resisting if we try to move his head in our hands. He can hold his head erect, or lift it up when lying prone. He will try to crawl when lying on his face, and roll over from his side to his back —or even from his back to his stomach. He will push hard with his feet on his mother's lap, and try to sit up. He has long been kicking vigorously in his bath, and will splash about with threshing movements of his arm. He can pick things up with his whole hand, " the palmar scoop ", although not yet with his fingers ; and can put his hand to his mouth almost as he wishes.

At nine months, the child has quite a varied repertory of controlled movements. He has long been able to sit up independently, and may now try to stand with help, and even to put one foot in front of another. He can now pick things up with his finger and thumb opposed, will scribble with a pencil imitatively, and already shows whether he is right- or left-handed. He will probably be able to say " ma-ma " and " da-da ". At the end of the year, he may be able to pronounce one or two other words, to crawl vigorously in any direction he wants, to climb up the side of his cot, and to walk with very little help, or even alone. He can use his fingers together in such a way as to put small bricks into a box, or to build one or two on top of another ; and he will scribble spontaneously if given pencil and paper.

**Play.** How much delight and interest his movements bring to him can be seen by anyone who watches either the two-months baby kicking in his bath, the nine-months-old cooing and gurgling and babbling as he makes sound experiments with his mouth, or the twelve-months child who shouts with laughter when he has managed to balance a third brick on top of his two-brick tower. And if we watch closely, we can see this pleasure in movement changing and developing new aspects. There is the simple sensory delight in movement for its own sake, which remains a primary source of well-being and personal happiness if we don't stupidly shut it out for him—the joy of the older child in running and leaping, the delight of the dancer. And then there is the pleasure in doing something new or difficult, in having an aim and achieving it—learning to walk or stand, to pick up a brick or say a new word. It is through these experiences that the baby's mind grows. His efforts and successes and failures are as earnest and important to his mental life as those of the golfer, the business man, the engineer, the artist are to them.

The play that brings the child skill and knowledge has now amply begun. He will pick up a toy and drop it over and over again, or bang a spoon on his tray to make a loud noise, crowing with delight as he does it.

**Play and language.** As we have seen, he plays with his voice too, repeating sounds over and over as he slowly masters them; and imitating sounds made by others. He finds that cries will bring his mother to him, and that cooing and gurgling will make her smile. He thus discovers the social value of the sounds he makes; and presently, begins to connect particular sounds with particular effects, and to know these sounds when others make them. He distinguishes an angry voice, a sad voice and a cheerful one—just as he is learning to know the smile from the frown, and to smile and frown in return. Soon he comes to use quite definite sounds to express definite desires and feelings; and language proper begins.

Throughout the later months of the first year, we can watch the child coming to recognise more and more of the things around him, toys and places and people alike. And at the same time we can see the growth of playful curiosity about things and people, and of pleasure in trying out this and that—shaking the rattle, watching mother come and go, looking at the fire or the lamp, splashing about in the bath, and so on.

**One year old.** The year-old child is an active, inquiring creature, who can get about the world a little, can poke things and pull them about to see what they're like, can move them in ways that interest him. He sits up and looks round alertly. He moves his eyes about for things to interest him, reaches out his hands to touch and pick up a spoon or a brick put near him, crawls or walks to get what is out of reach, calls out for help or attention, listens attentively and with recognition to approaching footsteps or voices, laughs with pleasure at a well-known face and looks with solemn inquiry at a stranger. And all this vast growth in the skill and purposiveness of his movements has come about in the short space of one year.

Let us now go back to the babe at birth and try to see what his inner life may be like.

**The suckling.** At birth, the babe is adapted to his mother in his mental life, rather than to the outside world. Can we discern what his mother seems to him? She cannot well be what we should mean by a *person*. She must seem to him hardly more than a nourishing breast and sheltering arms, a vague large *Something* which comforts and caresses and feeds him.

Mental life does not wait to begin until eyes and ears and active movement are bringing the outside world to the child, but is already active at the breast, and centred in his experiences there. While sight and hearing are undeveloped, and the movements of the limbs are weak and random, the food canal, and at first the mouth, loom large in the mind. The infant is a feeding animal, a suckling in mind as well as body. His mouth is his most sensitive part, and to it belong his most urgent and intense feelings. If we watch the voracious nuzzling of the breast, and the sharp turning away from things that taste or feel unpleasant to the mouth, *things that are not the breast*, we get a glimpse of how vivid and how much at the centre of his mental life the feelings and impulses of the mouth must be to the babe. If things that can be touched are the most real things in infancy, then things that can be touched *by the lips*, or, indeed, swallowed, are the most real things of all to the babe of the very earliest days.

The mouth is thus not only the means of getting nourishment, but also of the babe's first knowledge of the world outside himself. For a long time, everything his hand can reach is brought into his mouth. He not only eats, but thinks with his mouth.

**The babe and his mother.** Not only so : we can see too that the babe *loves* with his mouth, and feels his mother's love in her gift of the breast. His affectionate pleasure in the touch of the breast can be seen in his play with it after the first sharp pangs of hunger are satisfied. He will then suck a little, let the nipple slide out of his mouth, smile and gurgle and kick his legs with delight, then turn back and caress the nipple again with his lips. But if the mother withdraws the breast, how quickly the picture changes ! His face puckers and reddens, he screams with distress and anger, his fists clench and his body stiffens in protest. If then the nipple is returned to him, his body relaxes, the puckers fall away, he sighs or grunts in relief, and the busy mouth begins again to satisfy his hunger for nourishment and love. To give the breast is to the babe's mind in these early days to give love ; to withdraw or withhold it is to withdraw or withhold love. When we understand this, we see also how important are the ways in which we manage all the business of feeding and weaning.

**Biting.** Towards the second half of the year, a new phase of the infant's mental life begins to set in, with the first development of the teeth. His mouth impulses begin to change from sucking to biting—a more active and destructive way of dealing with things. He bites and chews everything that he can get to his mouth, his own finger or his mother's, a spoon, a toy, and the breast itself, if weaning has not yet been carried through. His pleasure in biting becomes as great as his enjoyment of sucking formerly was, and as natural a means of expressing his affection and desire. Most babies bite the nipple playfully as a primitive form of love, although this readily passes over into anger if the mother takes the nipple away. We usually meet this need to bite by giving the babe a hard ring to practise his teeth on, and we can see how much he enjoys it. With the onset of the biting impulses, the child has entered a new and important phase of his development.

**Fear and rage.** Apart from his breast experiences, there are two other ways in which we can call out strong emotions in the very young babe. If the arms that are holding him are suddenly loosened or lowered, or the blanket on which he is lying is suddenly twitched; or if there should be a sudden loud noise—the banging of a door, or the dropping of a tray—he will show every sign of sharp fear, particularly if at the time he is dozing. These are the two situations which call out immediate fear in the tiny infant. On the other hand, if we hold the babe's head firmly in our hands so that he cannot move it, or grip his arms very tightly and hold them still, he will show every symptom of acute but helpless rage. Later on, when he has wider perceptions and interests, such anger will tend to appear if he is thwarted in other ways; but in the beginning, it is called out by this forcible stopping of his movements. Against this, he will protest with all his might.

**The bowel.** Very early, moreover, the changes in the lower end of the digestive canal begin to secure the child's interest. The distension of the lower bowel by waste matter, and the movements made in passing this out, are definite organic experiences which draw his attention. Again, we have to look at this as an experience, and not simply as a matter of bodily hygiene.

In the very earliest days, the circular muscles controlling the exit are quite relaxed like most of the other muscles of the body. Soon they begin to gain some tone, and to relax only at intervals, this going along with the rhythmic spasms of the lower bowel, which force the bolus of fæces down and out. The babe finds pleasure in these rhythmic movements, as later in the other movements of the body. We can often observe the pleasure in actual expulsion which the baby feels, if we watch him closely. Even at eight or nine months, he will sometimes gurgle and grunt and smile and wriggle when he is evacuating, with as many signs of enjoyment as when someone he knows smiles at him or dangles something bright in front of his eyes.

As the tonicity of the sphincters increases, and discharge begins to take place less frequently, say at the normal interval of a day, there is a certain amount of distension of the lower bowel with the accumulated fæces. Up to a certain point this local pressure yields a pleasurable feeling, and some children show a tendency to retain the fæces for the sake of the heightened pleasure. Very often, of course, constipation begins through mistakes in feeding or changes in the mother's milk or other physiological cause. But occasionally a quite young infant may show a strong tendency to retain the stool, and consequently suffer in health, when there does not seem to be any definite reason in his food and drink. If we follow through the later development of such children, we usually find that they tend to be self-willed and obstinate all round. The tendency to constipation will often show itself all through childhood, along with these traits of character. Other children will tend to a looseness of the bowels right through their infancy and childhood, and these children will generally be found more generous and affectionate in character. It is the fact that definite traits of character very often go along with types of bowel behaviour that compels us to realise that the bowel processes are not just bodily affairs in the young child, but also have important mental aspects.

Very early indeed, as every mother knows, the bowel and bladder behaviour of the infant gets taken up into his general feeling relations with his mother or nurse. He soon becomes aware that we are pleased when he discharges the stool at the time and place we wish. We show this in all our ways of encouraging bowel movement, such as putting him on the pot and showing our relief in voice and smile when he uses it. He thus learns to give up the stool to please us, and may withhold it to assert himself or defy us. (Folk wisdom has long recorded the observation that a baby will pass his water while on the lap of someone he likes.) In training the babe in habits of cleanliness and regularity, then, we are never dealing with just a local mechanism. The standards we set and the ways we adopt will have far-reaching effects on his feeling towards us, and thus on his later social development.

**The babe's impatience.** It will help us further to

understand what is happening if we now look at the general character of the infant's behaviour in these early months.

Watching his earliest cries and struggles to get what he wants, his anger when he does not succeed at once, and his pleasure when he does, we can see how urgent and compelling his desires are, and how hardly he suffers delay. He wants what he wants here and now, and he wants it with the whole of himself. We sometimes express this by saying that his behaviour has an " all-or-none " quality. It is not finely graded to a particular situation, but, as it were, explodes to it. Those native reflex movements which we share with the babe, such as the blink of the eye when anything comes suddenly near, or the knee-jerk, always have this quality. We can't do them more or less ; if they happen at all, they happen fully. They are thus very different from the learned movements of skill, e.g. the delicate, finely-graded action of the tennis player, or from the tempered expression of emotion in most adults. With the very young infant, all his feelings and behaviour seem to be of this all-or-none type. And we can see that this must be so ; for as yet he knows nothing of time, and has no past or future wherewith to temper the here and now of desire. Delay must thus seem to him an absolute refusal. He is aware only of the absence of what he wants, not of its coming presently. For the mother, his cries mean " He is hungry, *and* I'm soon going to feed him ". For him, just " I want, and I haven't got ". Hence his distresses must be far more intense than ours and the contrast of his comfort far greater. And because of his inability to bear thwarting at this stage, his mother becomes to him the source, not only of his comfort and happiness, but also of his first denials and fears and disappointments.

The way in which the infant is given up to the feeling of each moment, as it comes and goes, is well illustrated in the following observations : " Bubi " (aged 5½ months) " was in his perambulator, and as we were busy reading he was left to his own devices, to amuse himself with his toy ; but evidently this did not suit him, the toy was thrown aside, and the boy looked at us expectantly. Since we did not move, he began to argue the matter. ' Tae, agga, atta-ava, mamm ham.' No result. Then he uttered short groans, drew his body up obstinately, threw himself suddenly forward, and, stiffening himself, fell back again directly, giving in these movements the impression of incredible wilfulness. As yet we did not respond, we suddenly heard a prolonged squeak on ' ee ', and there sat our son with a purple face and clenched fists, casting furious looks at us with his half-closed eyes, whilst he made mighty efforts to continue his hoarse never-ending ' ee ' squeak ! Then, when at last he was lifted out, quick as lightning his little face assumed an expression of contented gaiety and charming affection. The play of features was wonderfully varied, and expressed plainly and unmistakably the feelings mastering the child—anger, self-will, fear, defiance, disappointment." (From Scupin ; quoted by Stern, *Psychology of Early Childhood*, p. 126.)

Slowly, however, he becomes a shade less unmeasured in anger and desire, a shade more controlled in his impulses, as experience enters in and tempers them. He becomes able to remember a very little in this moment of anger how he felt a brief time ago in his passionate love ; and in this moment of loss and grief, how sometimes before what he desires has come back to him. He has begun to know the signs of coming satisfaction—at first, the touch and sight of his mother's arms, presently her step, her voice, or the preparations for the bath which may go before the feed. He is no longer left in an uncharted ocean of immediate desire, but has some guidance in former satisfactions and a foreseen future. All this comes about, however, very gradually and slowly.

We may now look at some of the practical suggestions arising from this brief outline of the infant's growth.

**The mother's patience.** In the first place, it is a help to us in dealing with babies and young children merely to know that even those things they do which seem undesirable to us may be normal ways of growth. To realise, for instance, that biting is an ordinary and general phase of development, and that all children at first take pleasure in those bodily processes which later on they and we feel to be disgusting, at once gives some relief to the anxious parent. He no longer feels quite so horrified when he finds his own infant being dirty, obstinate and angry ; and if he feels less disturbed about these things, he is able to deal with them more calmly and therefore more wisely. Children, and even young infants, are very sensitive to our anxiety about them, which shows itself even without our knowing it, in voice and gesture and touch. Watch the always anxious mother and her children—you will see that they do in fact give her more cause to be anxious than the children of a calmer, more serene mother, who is not so worried by the childishness of children, and not in such a hurry to make them behave like grown-ups. And the same children of the worried mother will give little or no trouble to another woman who is cool and confident. With time for their development, and the sense of our cheerful confidence, children will grow out of the behaviour most of us worry about.

If we can really get into our bones, so to speak, the sense of the slow growth of the infant's mind through these various bodily experiences, and the knowledge that each phase has its own importance in his development, we are more likely to give him the gentle care and patient friendliness which he most needs to carry him on successfully from one phase to the next, and to avoid the harsh and hasty methods which may make him fear and hate us. For this is the surest way to bind him in his infantile ways. The child who goes in fear of scoldings and naggings cannot expand freely and happily into social life. He is thrown back on the infant's mode of gaining love by his helplessness, or driven into the blind protest of rage and tantrums. It is now common knowledge among humane parents that fear of whippings or severe punishments has this evil effect, but it is not yet widely realised that the fear of carpings and harsh criticism may be just as paralysing to the sensitive child. He can most easily learn to fit himself into the social world if he is free from undue anxiety about possible mistakes, and has a sense of affectionate unity with those around him. As has been recently said, " The more a child's development comes about through its interests and affections rather than through moral training, the less sharp are the unavoidable conflicts and their consequences " (Dr. Ernest Jones, *Psycho-analysis*, 1928, p. 57).

**The biting child.** We are now able to make some answer to our questions about the child who bites. We can see that because a young child is given to biting either in playful affection or in anger, it does not follow that he is depraved or unusually cruel. All children do it to some extent and at some time or other. Even when a boy of four or five years still bites frequently and severely if he is thwarted or angry, it does not mean that he will necessarily go on doing so as he gets older. It certainly means that he has for some reason got held up in his development, and has retained a mode of anger and defence normal to the infant. As we should expect, we commonly find that most such children are unusually intolerant of any denial or disappointment. But it is certain that any form of severe punishment for the biting will not only fail to remedy this deep disturbance of development, but will fix the child more firmly still in his primitive mental ways. Yet equally clearly we cannot let him hurt or frighten other children.

What we can do, whenever we are near the quarrelling children, or when he tries to bite us, is actually to prevent him from biting by holding him away. We can say " I will not let you hurt Mary ", " I won't let you bite me ", without suggesting that his wish to bite is wicked or horrible. If we only come upon the scene when the harm has already been done, our sympathy and attention to the injured child is itself—provided we have not already spoilt our relation with the attacking child by previous severities and clumsinesses—a very considerable penalty. A matter-of-fact refusal to let him hurt others is usually enough : for his sense of isolation when he sees the sympathy which the other child's distress calls out in us is indeed so strong that we may have soon to reassure him of our love. The tendency to bite will, of course, be affected by our general attitudes towards him ; and if, in general, he feels that we understand his need for power and self-assertion, although we prefer him to express these in ways which will not injure others, he is more likely to become free of his primitive modes of feeling and behaving, than if we constantly check and punish him.

So with the babe who begins to bite the nipple. If we punish him actively, by smacking or sharply scolding, as a matter of course we make him feel the more angry and aggressive. In smacking him we are ourselves seeming cruel to him. A boy of four years known to me, one of the most hostile and unhappy children imaginable, had been smacked by his mother when a baby for playfully biting the nipple. The mother believed that " You couldn't begin training too early " ; but she did not realise that to smack the babe at the breast was to begin his training in cruelty and hasty anger. The gentle withdrawal of the nipple when the child bites is a sufficient hint to him that he cannot have his mother if he hurts her.

**Feeding and weaning.** Again, what has been said about suckling from the point of view of the child's feelings towards his mother will have made clear that, for instance, to be late with a feed and keep the hungry child beyond his expected time is not *only* to leave him hungry, but also to disturb the rhythm of his love satisfactions. He cries not *only* because he is hungry, but also because he is lost without love, and love does not come to him. He can after the first few weeks adapt his expectations to regular feeding and tending, for this means a steady love which does not leave him a prey to the terrors of loss.

And we can see how great a crisis the experience of

weaning must be, if it comes too early or too suddenly. To give the bottle or spoon instead of the breast makes feeding a cold and heartless thing, a mere affair of satisfying hunger, and no longer a way of enjoying close contact with the mother.   If it happens before the child has so far developed in mind that his mother is much *more* than the breast to him, before he can feel her love satisfyingly in, for instance, her voice and smile and ways of response to his active play, then to lose the breast means to lose love, and is inevitably a great personal shock.   If the change be sudden, the child cannot immediately find different ways of comfort, and suffers severely in his inner life.   Whereas if he has been used to drink water from the spoon since his early weeks, so that this has already become part of the loving attention given to him, and the sensations and movements it brings are not strange ;  if the change over from breast to bottle and spoon is gradual, so that he has time to get used to it ;  if it comes in the third quarter of his year of infancy, so that he has enjoyed a normal satisfaction of his impulses towards the breast, and his development now makes it possible for him to understand other signs of his mother's love, and so to feel sure that this is not lessened *although* the breast is withdrawn, then he is likely to accept the change with little difficulty. Children differ, however, in the ease with which they can accept it, and we need to watch their responses and graduate the time and rate of the change to their personal needs.   There is thus reason to think that too early a complete weaning should be avoided, unless there are very strong reasons for it on grounds of bodily health ; and that it should be done as gradually as possible, with due care for the child's happiness as well as his diet.

**Handling the infant.** Then again, how important our ways of handling him, of dressing and undressing, and the ease or tightness of his garments are bound to be ! When we put him into clothes that are tight and uncomfortable or take an unnecessarily long time to get on and off, we are not merely reddening his skin and giving him less air and exercise for his body. We are violating his fundamental impulses, the impulses by which his mind develops. And we are showing ourselves to him as persons who restrict and anger him. He can only know us by what we do to him. He has no other vital contact with our minds. *We* may feel that we love him ; but if we startle him by sudden noises or by clumsy handling, if we worry him by tight clothing, it cannot seem so to him !

**Training in cleanliness.** So with his training in cleanliness and regular habits of bowel and bladder. We need to be gentle here too, not putting our standards too rigidly high, nor making our own immediate convenience the first consideration. It is undoubtedly wise to give the infant an opportunity of regular habits from the earliest days, by putting him on a vessel after each feed ; and a calm patience at the beginning will often save greater difficulties of training at a later stage. But while giving the opportunity, we must not be distressed if every child does not respond at once, and must not spend too much time over it. We must remember that the baby *is* a baby, and not expect him to behave as a child of ten. Nor must we expect all children to behave alike at the same age. Some children accept our suggestions of time and place far more easily than others, and whilst this is very convenient for us, it does not follow that these docile infants are the ones who will

develop the most satisfactorily in every respect, nor be
the most valuable persons socially when they are grown
up. Indeed, there are many grounds for feeling distressed about the too-clean and too-docile child, even in
these earliest days ; for he may suffer, in ways that lead
to mental illness, under the strain of accepting adult
standards too early. In general, what we expect of him
must be graded to what he can in fact succeed in. We
must look for his growth, and not for a miracle.

Sometimes the child who begins by responding very
easily to such regular suggestion, and seems to have
established regular ways during the first few months,
will later on, perhaps at the time when he begins to
walk, or at two and three years, be more irregular and
wilful. Just because these organic happenings belong to
the child's first ways of mental life, the first adjustments
are liable to be disturbed again when he feels a strong
impulse of self-assertion or defiance, or fear, or angry
disappointment with his parents, or jealousy about the
birth of another child, or a wish to draw attention to
himself (even if it be a scolding). We need not, however,
be very worried about this as an occasional happening.
If the child is developing normally, such phases will pass
even without our scoldings and penalties—and, indeed,
all the more readily without them. For if we pay too
much attention to occasional lapses, the child feels too
guilty about them, and fears their happening again ;
and the very fear lessens his control and hastens the
dreaded accident. A simple suggestion, not implying
any disapproval, that he should help us to make him
clean again, is as far as it is wise to go. In general, our
aim should be to lessen the emotional element in the
whole process, and to develop a matter-of-fact attitude

towards it, in the child and in ourselves. (It is best, for instance, to leave the child, after infancy, alone during his morning visit to the lavatory, and encourage him to manage things for himself as soon as possible.) The key-note to the whole problem (as to most problems of early childhood) is to avoid forcing early compliance with our wishes through the motive of fear, and to wait patiently and confidently until the child's developing affection for us leads him to offer it freely.

**Thumb-sucking.** Another acute problem arising in later infancy or soon after is that of thumb-sucking. The pleasure which the baby gains from the movements of his mouth is shown very clearly in the way in which he commonly takes to sucking his thumb as a substitute for the nipple. With some babies this begins within the first few days, with others not until later ; and a few children seem never to do it at all. A great many nurses and doctors feel as strong a disapproval about this spontaneous discovery of the infant as they do about the old and dishonoured practice of seducing him with a dummy. They will go almost any lengths in the attempt to break off the " habit ".

Before allowing ourselves to make the child unhappy in our efforts to prevent this, however, we need to be very clear as to its disadvantages, if any, and the equally possible disadvantages of our methods of breaking it.

Undoubtedly if the baby sucks his thumb vigorously all the time, the thumb may get sore or dwarfed, and the shape of the mouth be affected. This great excess is, however, quite rare, and we should not attribute its evils to an occasional or slight amount of sucking the thumb, particularly in the young baby when he is comforting himself to sleep. When it does occur to this excess, it sometimes means that the child has not been getting properly satisfied at the breast, or that his general feeding arrangements need altering in some details which can be found out by observation. It should, in fact, be treated rather as a symptom than as a mere " habit ".

If he does it only when he is falling to sleep, or even sometimes for a short time when awake, it is not likely to do any particular harm. We all tend to feel much more anxious about it than we really need be, for most babies whose conditions of food and sleep are satisfactory grow out of it as their general interests widen and grow more lively.

If we notice its happening in the very early days, we may be able to prevent its settling into a habit by placing the baby's arms in his wraps in such a way that he cannot easily get his hand to his mouth unless he is very determined. But we have to remember that if he *is* very determined, that is to say, if the need for this form of satisfaction is very urgent, then the persistent sense of helpless irritation which we induce in him by tying his arms down or by putting his hands into mittens is far more likely to be harmful than the thumb-sucking itself. This is what is so often forgotten by those who advocate severe measures to " break the habit ". They forget that the baby is not a machine, with no life of its own, in which this, that or the other part can be moved just at *our* will. We *can* prevent the baby getting his thumb to his mouth—but sometimes only at the price of continued nervous strain and helpless anger, which spreads most harmfully over the whole mental life.

If we want to help the confirmed thumb-sucker of the middle or later months of this year to grow out of the habit, we must first of all assure ourselves that he is getting full satisfaction of hunger at the breast or bottle, and that he is not deprived of his legitimate time of pleasurable love play with the nipple before he is put down to sleep.

For the toddler or the older child it is also a great help to give a substitute pleasure in the shape of a good boiled sweet. Not of course just when the child is going to sleep, but after he gets into bed, before he is finally tucked up. This will make it a little easier for him to do without his thumb.

After this, we may turn our attention to weaning his interest from the thumb during his waking hours, not by negative methods of prevention, but by giving him more companionship in play than would otherwise be necessary. Such a child should be left lying alone in his cot when awake much less than one who does not find his interest in his own thumb. We may talk to him more often, share his fun in watching the trees or coloured streamers blow in the wind, in listening to his rattle, in raising himself up and pushing his feet against our lap, in picking up and throwing down his spoon and bricks, and in all his general play and his developing interests in the outer world. This companionship in outwardly directed interests undoubtedly helps to deprive the thumb of its special value as a source of pleasure. And it quite avoids all the harmful effects of negative measures.

**Companionship.** In general, what the infant during his first year needs other than the food and sleep and air and sunshine which the modern science of child-rearing finds for him, are freedom to play and things to play with ; and, towards the end of the year, some

companionship in play. In the earliest months the
babe spends the greater part of his life in sleep ; but
as the days go by, he is awake and receptive for longer
periods. In the middle months of this first year, he will
lie contentedly alone, looking at the sky or the moving
trees, or watching his own fingers as he twists and turns
them, and crooning to himself. But towards the end
of the year, he begins to show, along with his growing
power of interest in the world, a keener desire for active
human companionship, the stimulus of voices and
laughter and the pleasure of sharing pleasures.

It is important to realise this, for since medical opinion
began to stress the inestimable value of sleep and quiet
for the young child, there has been a growing tendency
for intelligent mothers, wishing to act according to the
strict tenets of modern hygiene, to leave the baby lying
in his cot alone, for long hours, so that he should be
encouraged to sleep as much as possible. This is probably the wisest thing in the early months ; and even
later on, as a general policy. But it is being carried
too far, if it means, as it sometimes does, that the child
has his mother with him only when she is feeding or
bathing him or perhaps for short periods at prescribed
intervals, and that at all other times he is expected to lie
in his pram, whether or not he is feeling lively and eager.

Not only so : there is a common idea about the year-old
baby, and even about the toddler of two or three years,
that he *ought* to be willing to " amuse himself " and play
alone. If he does not, he is considered tiresome and
naughty. There is, however, no basis for this notion in
the facts of the child's development. Most one-year-olds
seek actively for the companionship of a grown-up in
their play.

To deprive the child of human society when he is ready for it on any such view or on some rigid theory about inducing him to sleep by hook or by crook, is a serious educational mistake. It leaves him bored and irritated. It throws him back on the primitive pleasures of sucking his fingers or rocking his body, and baffles his first spontaneous movements towards social life. I have known more than one child whose social development was held back by this starvation of early delight in companionship, in the later months of the first year and the beginning of the second. One extremely intelligent child who was always left alone in his pram, apart from actual meal and bath times, took refuge partly in a rocking movement of the whole body, which persisted as a nervous habit well into childhood ; and partly in a too-frequent wish to urinate. " Ah-ah ! " he would say, at short intervals, knowing that this would cause him to be taken up and attended to, and thus give him the companionship he sought, at least for a brief time.

This is but a further illustration of the general point that we must not apply even the soundest doctrine too rigidly, without a day-by-day regard for the actual needs of the particular children we are dealing with, at their particular stage of growth.

CHAPTER IV

## NORMS OF DEVELOPMENT

A GE and growth. We have seen in our study of
the infant in his first year how closely the growth
of the child's mind is bound up with the growth of his
body. We have seen, too, that growth is much more
than a mere increase in size and vigour. To the body,
it brings changes in the relative proportion and the ways
of functioning of limbs and organs ; to the mind, changes
in actual experience, in practical skills, in the meanings
of things and the directions of interest.

We can, therefore, hope to discover in general a definite
relation between the age of a child and the stage of
growth he has reached. And one of our tasks in trying
to understand him is to trace out this relation in detail,
so as to see what his particular needs are at any particular age. The study of the characteristic development
of skill and interests through the successive years of
childhood is of great practical value to parents and
educators.

One of the everyday problems noticed in our first
chapter, for instance, raised the question of the age
at which a child should be allowed to feed herself.
Young mothers sometimes seem to fear that the child's
wish to be independent at an early age is " precocious "
and perhaps a little perverse. " If she is allowed to

try to feed herself, won't it simply mean that she will just play about all the time, not getting enough to eat, taking much longer over meals, and thus upsetting all practical arrangements ?  Ought the child not to be content to accept her food meekly from a grown-up ? " Or again, a little girl of twenty months is very eager to wash her own hands, too.  She likes the sight and feel of soapsuds, and cries stormily when the nurse lifts her away from them and insists on drying her hands. So much does she want to wash her hands herself that within a few minutes she will dirty them again in the coal box, and come to the nurse saying, " Hands dirty —wash."  The mother is inclined to feel that she ought to treat this as a case of disobedience and punish the child ; but fortunately a doubt creeps into her mind as to whether this is real perversity, or whether perhaps, after all, children of twenty months could not learn to wash their own hands.

The same sort of question arises about the child's learning to dress himself, and the age at which we can expect him to control his bladder and bowels.  The practical value of knowing something of the normal age for all these things is obvious.  If a mother understands what a child of any given age can reasonably be expected to do for himself, when he can be expected to feed himself, wash himself, put on his own shoes and button his coat, build with bricks or throw a ball, learn to read and write, use Meccano or play football, she will be able to avoid, on the one hand, spoiling the child by treating him too much as a baby, and on the other, demanding more from him than he can really achieve, and so making him fretful and impatient.

Another practical issue which raises the question of

age is that of play material. " What sort of toys should I give my little boy who is just two ? Is he old enough to have plasticine or bricks ? "

It is clearly desirable to give children play material suited to their stage of development. This will help their growth and keep them happily content. Toys that are either too " childish " or too advanced, and so fail to stir the children's active interests, waste more than our money.

These illustrations open up for us the whole problem of *age-norms* of development, a general question which it will be useful to discuss before carrying our detailed study of children beyond the year of infancy.

**Age-norms.** How can we find out what the special needs of children are at particular ages ? How have psychologists discovered them ?

Simply by observing in detail what very many children do and say at different ages and in varied situations. The intelligence and the interests of children alike are expressed in their behaviour with limbs and tongue.

The question is in its essence on all fours with the problem of age-norms in height and weight. We all know how the regular daily and weekly weighing of an infant has become an ordinary part of infant care. The loss or gain of weight is an indispensable guide to the babe's health, and the sure test of a particular way of feeding or living.

But before we could use the change in weight of any particular child under particular conditions as a way of judging his health and the wisdom of his diet, we had to study the general growth in weight of a very large number of children of all ages under different conditions. That is to say, we had to find out the average or *norm* of weight at any given age, and the average or normal *rate of increase* in weight from year to year. Only when we had this normal curve of increase in weight to go by, could we tell whether this, that or the other child was putting on weight " as he should ", or was perhaps under- or over-weight for his age. What we mean when we say he " should " be of such-and-such a weight is that that is the average or normal weight for a child of his age. And the average has been arrived at by measuring a great many individual children.

In just the same way, psychologists have been engaged for many years in trying to discover the normal mode and rate of growth of the mind throughout childhood. This is, of course, a much more difficult problem than the study of growth in bodily height and weight. Mental growth is very varied and complex. It shows itself in so many different ways, and is so intimately affected by many varied influences, that it is far from easy to find really reliable ways of measuring it and of discovering its general laws. Great progress has, however, been made, and it is now comparatively easy for any trained psychologist to measure the mental development of a child at any age, and to say whether he is up to the normal, or how far and in what way he differs from it. And we can do this, not only for general growth in intelligence as a whole, but also for particular directions of growth such as language, drawing, manipulative skill, or reasoning.

Mothers and nurses and teachers are, of course, always making use of the *notion* of a " norm " of growth. Every time they talk of how " Mary was slow in learning to speak ", " Tommy walked very early ", " Jane is backward in her letters " or " Joan is very forward at dressing herself ", they are obviously referring to the idea of the *norm* for these things. The difference between this everyday use of the notion of normal development and that resulting from the work of the psychologist is just a difference of exactitude. The trained student can now say much more *exactly* how far a child is behind or ahead of the normal for his age and how far he has advanced during any given year of development.

It is obviously very important that we should be able to measure the rate of mental growth exactly if we are to find out what those things are which affect it. If we want to know, for example, what the real effect of a particular method of training is, whether a child grows more favourably when he has other children to play with or is left alone, whether the solitary child is handicapped in his growth, whether bodily disturbance, such as a long illness or a glandular deficiency, may affect mental growth, and all the other things it would be so useful to know, we obviously need to be able to measure the rate of mental growth accurately and reliably. Mere rough and ready comparisons made by anybody will hardly help us to judge the value of different ways of training, or to come to any final conclusions about the best conditions of growth.

**Mental tests.** The observations or simple experiments by means of which we study and record the interests and skill of children of different ages are often spoken of as " mental tests ".

Mental tests are thus simply scientific ways of (*a*) finding out the normal course of mental development among children generally—with regard to all such details as learning to walk and talk, the development of speech, of skill of hand and eye, of ability to draw, of counting and number, of reasoning, etc.; (*b*) measuring the growth of any particular child, to see whether he is up to the " norm " for his age, behind it or beyond it; and (*c*) distinguishing between inborn ability and the effects of training.

One of the first psychologists to use the concept of age-norms and to try to discover actual norms by exact methods was a French student of children, Alfred Binet. His scale of tests for the measurement of intelligence at succeeding ages is the best known and perhaps the most widely used. Binet's work has been carried further and adapted to English-speaking children by many other psychologists, notably Burt in this country, and Terman in America. As, however, Binet's tests are concerned chiefly with children of five years and over (they do include tests for three- and four-year-olds, but these are nothing like so reliable as those for older children), we need not speak of them further here.

Perhaps the most important work on norms of development for infants and young children is being done by Gesell [1] at the Yale Psychological Clinic in America. In his laboratory and nursery school Gesell has made a very full and detailed study of the development of movement and skill from birth onwards amongst a great many children. Every sort of scientific device is being used for observing, recording and photographing the behaviour of infants and little children, both in their spontaneous play and in response to actual tests.

One important condition which Gesell has found a way of providing for is that the children should be observed without their knowing. If they are aware that

[1] See books quoted for reference.

they are being watched, of course they often behave differently. Gesell, therefore, uses a most ingenious observation screen, which is opaque in one direction and transparent in another. The child who is being studied plays inside this screen, and can thus be seen without himself seeing the observer. He plays either alone, with other children, or with a grown-up experimenter who gives him little problems to solve with hand and eye. And both the material and the method of giving these problems are themselves carefully standardised so as to be the same for all the children tested. The experimenter notes the movement of the infant's fingers as he picks up a pellet, the number of bricks a two-year-old child can pile up one on top of another, how quickly the three-year-old will fit a series of differently shaped blocks of wood into the right holes in a form-board, or arrange the pieces of a picture puzzle ; and so on and so forth. Meanwhile, the movements, expressive gestures and facial expressions of the child can be watched and faithfully recorded in detail by another observer, who is outside the screen and thus invisible to the child himself ; or still more accurately by a camera. (This special screen, moreover, makes it possible not only for the psychologists, but also for the children's parents, to watch the children's play without their knowledge. In this way the parents sometimes learn a lot that is new and very revealing about their children, as I shall suggest in regard to feeding problems later on.)

**Cross-sections of growth.** With these and other scientific aids Gesell has made the most fascinating records of the typical stages of development of children from birth to five or six years.

He has made detailed comparisons of the skill and the social responses of the one-month infant with the two-months, the two with the three, the five with the six, and so on, thus creating a series of cross-section pictures of development which bring out the directions of change most clearly. And after building up the general normative summaries of growth for each successive month and year, he has then gone on to study the individual ways in which particular children differ from the general characteristics for any given age, and the possible sources of such difference. The whole of Gesell's work is of the greatest interest to all students of children, as my readers would see at once if they turned to his photographs illustrating characteristic periods of development.

In studying the infant in his first year of life, I described the details of his growth in movement and skill from month to month. I might now take the characteristic growth of the child during his second year as an illustration of the general meaning of norms of development, and of their practical significance.

**Development in the second year.** What sort of things can the average child of just twelve months do? He can walk with more or less help, and lower himself from a standing to a sitting position. He can hold a pencil sufficiently well to make a mark or scribble, and will imitate on a piece of paper a scribble made by another person. If his mother rattles a spoon in a cup, the twelve-months baby will do the same. If a bright-coloured bone ring he is interested in is placed beyond his reach, but with a string attached to it within his reach, he will pull the string so as to get at the ring. If we take a wooden cube he is playing with, and wrap it up in tissue paper and give it back to him, he will unwrap the paper to get at the cube. At this age, he can as a rule say two words besides " mama " and " dada ", and understand a good many more, as will be shown by his doing things he is told to do, such as clap his hands or hide them away. He will wave " Bye-bye " and can often say it. If he is asked to put his wooden cube into a cup, without any gesture being made for him to imitate, he will do so. The average child of twelve months, too, can hold a cup to drink from, and will help to dress himself by holding his arms or legs appropri-ately. He will inhibit simple acts when told to, for example, if he is told not to touch something placed in front of him. If he does something that makes the people round him laugh, he will do it again to make them laugh once more.

Now let us see what development takes place in the following months. The average fifteen-months child, for instance, will walk alone and stand alone quite freely. He will now be able to build a tower of two blocks high. If he is holding two cubes in his hand and a third is placed in front of him, he will reach and take hold of the third without dropping the other two. (At an earlier age he would usually drop one of the first two in order to pick up the third.) He can now usually say four words besides " mama " and " dada ", and will often talk most expressively in a sort of jargon—all sorts of syllables and words tumbling out without any ideas attached, but all in the most expressive and varied tones of voice, as if the child really were carrying on an animated conversation. Again, the child of this age can use a spoon to a certain extent, and co-operates still more effectively in being dressed.

At eighteen months, he can climb on to a chair or up a flight of not too high stairs. He can throw a ball into a box and build a tower of three or more bricks high. He will now take four or more cubes without dropping those he already has, and when asked, he will put a cube *either* into a cup or a plate, as instructed. With chalk and board or with paper and pencil he will scribble freely and with delight, and if one sits beside him and makes a stroke oneself, he will imitate and make another. When asked, he will point to his eyes, nose or hair, showing that he clearly understands what is meant by those names ; and he will himself use five or more words. He will still enjoy making an imaginary conversation with a jumble of sounds, words and syllables. He can now (on the average) use a spoon successfully to feed himself. He will turn the pages of a book and look at pictures. He will try to put his own shoes on, although rarely with success. He will imitate the dramatic gestures of other people in play, with laughter and enjoyment.

The twenty-one months child can walk alone for considerable distances, and can walk backwards as well as forward (which means a great advance in poise and control of the limbs). If we build with his bricks a tower and a bridge beside each other, he will show that he appreciates the difference between them, although he cannot yet build the bridge imitatively. If we make first a stroke and then a scribble for him to imitate, he will see the difference and respond appropriately. He can as a rule give the name of at least one picture of a common object, and can use simple sentences of two words. At this age he will often repeat things said by other people although not necessarily understanding them. He will now ask for things he wants at the meal table or in the lavatory. He will try to turn a door-knob, and will pull his mother or nurse by skirt or hand in order to show her something he wants her to see, or to get for him. His bowel control is now well established.

At the end of this year, at the twenty-four months level, the child can do a great many more things, and do them much more skilfully, than he could at the beginning. He now not only walks, but runs. He can build a tower of six blocks with fair ease and balance. He will put bricks in a row to make a train, and play with them as if they were a train. If we fold a piece of paper with one crease in front of him and ask him to do one like it, he will imitate it quite easily. If when he has paper and pencil we make a vertical stroke and ask him to make one, he can do it. If we then make a horizontal stroke, he will imitate that too. (The horizontal strokes are apparently harder to make, and come later in development than vertical.) He will be able to name at least three familiar objects, such as a key, a penny and a watch, and to point to at least five simple pictures of objects (cup, ball, clock, etc.) when asked to do so by name. He will use many simple sentences and phrases if he is of average development in language. He will already enjoy stories as well as little dramatic games, and will tell others of what he has seen. He loves at this age to play with sand, filling and emptying buckets or jars. He can play simple catch and toss with a ball, and can manage a " Kiddie Car ". The control of his bladder is fairly well established at two years of age.

This, then, is the main outline of the average child's growth during his second year. Now let us look at some of the practical conclusions about playthings and ways of training which follow from these facts of development.

**Playthings.** At the beginning of this second year, the baby doesn't need many actual *things* to play with. His own limbs and his own mouth give him great fun. When he is awake he spends a lot of time " la-la-ing " and babbling, making different sorts of noises and saying over and over any actual words he knows, " mama ", " dada ", " din-din ", and so on. He gets lots of pleasure from waving his arms about, kicking his legs and trying to walk. At this age he loves to practise walking while he holds on to one finger or the skirt of a kind grown-up, or on to a chair that he pushes along. Lots of babies, however, still prefer to get about the floor by a sort of hitching movement while sitting on one leg, and very often if they hit upon this method they don't bother to try to walk except when a grown-up calls them from a few steps away, and someone else is there to give a helping finger. But they do love the mere joy of getting up and sitting down, and will shout with laughter about it. And then a little later they begin to toddle about, with unsteady steps that slowly grow more balanced and firm.

The busy mother or nurse can't be with her baby all the time. Yet she wants him to get all the exercise he can, and all the fun of moving about and crawling and trying to walk, and naturally doesn't want to strap him in his pram any more than she can help. On the other hand, she can't very well leave him free to crawl into any sort of danger or mischief. The best help she can have at this age is therefore a railed pen, strongly made, but light enough to be moved easily from one room to another, or better still, carried out to the garden when the sun is shining. With a soft rug on the floor, the baby is safe and comfortable inside the pen, and can lie and kick or crawl or try to walk to his heart's content.

Such a railed pen is not a very cheap thing, but it is very durable, and can of course be used for one child after another in the same family, or easily sold second-hand to other mothers when it is finished with. The other playthings that the child needs in this second year are so simple that their cost is next to nothing.

The baby in his pen will pull himself up by the side, chuckling with triumph, and sit down again with a bump that makes him laugh all the more, and do this over and over again. This sort of arm exercise is very good for him, both now and later on, taking his weight off the still soft bones of his legs. He will peep through the bars or try to look over the top and poke his finger through to touch his friend the dog, or to stroke the soft fur of Pussy as she arches her back and rubs up against the rail. He can have his own chair to sit on for a change, and his playthings beside him on the rug. And as the year goes on, the variety of his playthings can be added to from time to time.

Bright-coloured ribbons that will blow in the wind can be tied to the top of the rail. A large rattle will still amuse him. A hand-bell (if he is in the garden where the noise won't be too trying for other people) is great fun—or for that matter an old tin tray and a spoon to beat it with. He will love this and will crow with delight and the sense of power as he does it. We can't very well let him do it indoors. It is too trying to our own tempers. But out of doors in the garden he might be allowed to enjoy it, at any rate for short periods when he gets a little bored with other things.

Then he will love any sort of box, a cardboard shoe box, a bright-coloured box that has had Christmas presents in it, a round tin with a lid that he can take on and off, or a large wooden box that he can throw things into. There must be no splinters if the box is wooden ; no sharp corners or edges if it is tin (there are, however, plenty of round biscuit tins that are not sharp) ; and no pieces that he can easily pull off and chew if it is cardboard. But boxes of all sorts are a great delight at this age. The mere opening and shutting of the lid, dropping things in and tipping them out, seem to fascinate the child in his second year.

Then he wants things to put in the boxes and throw out again. A few wooden bricks of different sizes, but not smaller than a couple of inches square, a few large pebbles of different colours from the seashore, a few large shells of the sort that won't break easily. (All these smaller things must of course be too large to get into his mouth and be swallowed.) A smooth stick to poke through the railings or throw over the side is another treasure.

Clean silver sand or yellow sea sand in a box is greatly loved towards the end of this year and for several years to come. The child likes running it through his fingers, poking a stick into it, spooning it into an enamel mug with a wooden spoon, and pouring it out again. All these play movements help his arms and fingers to grow more skilful, as well as keep him contented. A year or two later dried beans make a very good plaything, but at this age he can't have them because he would put them in his mouth and swallow them.

Then a bright-coloured rubber ball or soft woollen ball, a rubber doll that squeaks when he hits or punches it, are much enjoyed. Another plaything that he will begin to enjoy towards the end of this year is a set of wooden rings which can be dropped or thrown on to a stick held upright in the sand or fixed in a round wooden base. Towards the end of this year too, he will get great fun out of a nest of boxes of different sizes, taking them out and fitting them in again to his heart's content.

As regards soft toys, dolls and animals, it is very important that these should not be hairy, for the baby is sure to put them to his mouth and chew them, and if the hair comes off he may easily choke with it or swallow it. This sort of toy can be expensive, but it isn't really necessary to buy the dear kind. Home-made ones are just as good. A doll or a rabbit or a cat can easily be made out of soft flannel stuffed with soft rags, and the baby will love this just as much as a more life-like imitation from the shop. A very simple soft doll can be quickly made from a hank of coloured wool tied round the neck and the middle and divided off for the legs and arms, with coloured beads sewn on for the eyes. Another thing that the one-year-old and even the two- or three-year-old adores is a large soft bag of coloured casement cloth to put his treasures in. A box of quite large coloured buttons amuses him too, but of course they must be too large to put into his mouth.

We must not forget the floating toys for the bath : a rubber doll, duck or fish. These are quite cheap, even with fast colours, which are of course essential since the infant is sure to suck them. And it is not only in his own bath that he will enjoy having them. In the summer, on a warm day, there is no better plaything in the world than a large pail or zinc bath of water. The baby can throw things in this to make an exciting splash, float his toy animals in it, or pour the water in and out of an enamel mug. He will of course have to wear mackintosh drawers, because he is quite sure to sit down on the place where he has just spilt some water. But his glee when he pours and splashes in this way is so great that so long as we can be sure he is not going to catch cold we can hardly give him anything that will keep him more happy and jolly.

Another thing that he will like and that gives him splendid exercise is a hassock. Towards the end of the year, if he could have two or three of different sizes which could be arranged like a stair, he would practise climbing up these and jumping off them over and over again.

These things need not be given all at once, of course. At the beginning of the year one or two things will keep the child happy ; for example, the pebbles and a box. But as he grows towards his second birthday, some of these other playthings can be added from time to time. The child gets bored with too much of the same thing, just as we do, and a variety of simple playthings gives him more fun and more things to learn to do.

**Doing things for himself.** All the babe's play with these things will help his arms and legs and fingers to grow more sure of themselves. Pouring the water and trying to carry a mug full of it without spilling, a game which he will enjoy if we teach it to him, will help him to manage his own cup and drink his milk at the table

without spilling it. His play in spooning up the sand
with a large wooden spoon or an ordinary teaspoon
will help him to manage his spoon at the table in feeding
himself. By the time he is fifteen months old he is very
likely to want to use his own spoon at the meal table.
If he does want to try, we should by all means let him
do so. He is sure to spill more or less in the beginning,
but he can't learn to manage it tidily unless he does
try. If we go the right way about it he will soon learn.
It is better not to scold or make a fuss if he does spill
a little, and better not to hold his hand while he is trying.
Babies hate that more than anything. They often fly
into a furious temper if their hands are held when they
are trying to spoon up the food for themselves. And
when they are in a furious temper they can't be taught
anything.

It would be better to let the child use the spoon for
one mouthful, and then the grown-up give him the
next, and so on alternately, until he sees how it is best
done. And it pays to make a game of it all, and to
praise him when he does well rather than to scold him
when he doesn't. By the time he is nineteen or twenty
months of age, if he has been allowed to try with help
and encouragement in this way, he will probably be
able to manage things very well.

But the sort of spoon and the sort of dish he has
make a great deal of difference. It should not be a
flat plate or even a shallow dish, because these make
it difficult to chase the food about with the spoon. A
deep dish or a basin are better. The spoon should
be small or he will stuff his mouth too full, but it should
have a deep bowl too, so that he can get the food up
easily with it. His drinking-mug too should be rather

small, but with a good-sized handle that he can hold firmly.   And when he is going to try to drink out of it by himself only a little fluid should be put in it at any one time.

If the child's mug and dish and spoon are put on an enamel tray and his chair is of a comfortable height, and the right nearness to the table, any mess he does make in learning to be independent can easily be swept up.

In this second year, even the brightest baby can hardly learn to dress himself, but if he is encouraged, he will already be beginning to help in the dressing by putting his arms in the right position, taking hold of his sock to help pull it on, and so on.   If we do everything for him without trying to start him off towards self-help, we get through the business of dressing and undressing much more quickly.   But we lose lots of fun on the way, and we waste our chance to train him to early independence.   We should let him help all he possibly can, and never check any movement he makes towards doing things for himself.   Even when he is being washed he will like to try to soap his own fingers and make a lovely lather.   Some children of twenty and twenty-two months can wash and dry their own hands with very little help, and like to practise doing it.

If the grown-ups take a little longer time over all these efforts at the beginning, and show their patience in helping and encouraging the child to do things for himself, many hours of needless waiting on him later on, as well as of bad temper, may be saved.   And the foundations of more complete independence as the child grows from year to year will have been laid.

We see, thus, that our young mother's anxious query

about her little girl's wish to feed herself is answered
by the fact that the average age for feeding oneself
reasonably well with a spoon is eighteen months. The
child's impulse to try was therefore healthy and normal.
To keep her dependent would but have hampered her
growth, and to call her " disobedient " because a true
growth impulse led her to keep reaching out for the
spoon and cry when it was denied her would surely
have been to twist all moral values out of focus.

**The precocious child.** Another important point can
be brought out of this same mother's query, one upon
which much light has been thrown by the study of norms
of development. The mother had feared that the child
was " precocious ", and she evidently shared a fairly
general notion that " precocity " is an undesirable thing.
There is still a widespread feeling among parents that
precocious children are bound to be " highly strung "
and " nervous ", and that they should be " kept back ".
In fact, however, this policy of " keeping back ", whether
in home or school, leads to nothing but boredom and
naughtiness.

The idea lingers on from the time when our general
methods of educating young children were very different
from what they commonly are to-day. It is a relic from
the days of mere blind cramming of facts into the
child's mind by methods that violated his needs and
nature.

When we taught children all the wrong things in all
the wrong ways, fine needlework, reading and writing
with fine materials, quantities of meaningless arithmetical
and grammatical facts, then the child who got on was
truly in danger of a nervous breakdown, since he could
only do well under the pressure of fear and whippings,

and his very well-doing brought an immense strain to his nervous system.

The matter is very different when our methods and conditions are better adapted to the child's normal modes of growth and spontaneous interests. If the child has ample opportunity for free play and bodily exercise, if his love of making and doing with his hands is met, if his intelligent interest in the world around him is encouraged by sympathy and understanding, if he is left free to make-believe or to think as his impulses take him, then his advances in skill and understanding are but welcome signs of mental health and vigour. If the " precocity " is spontaneous, and not the result of forced cramming, then it is one of the most desirable things in the world, for it simply means greater intelligence.

**Mental age.** We have only begun to understand this question of precocity, and the opposite one of backwardness, since we knew something of the normal modes and rate of mental development. It was, in fact, the problem of backwardness among school children, and its possible causes, that brought Binet and others to study the growth of intelligence and the way it shows itself at successive ages. And Binet's work led him to the notion of the *mental age*, the age which a child's mind has reached as compared with the average or norm of development for each year of chronological age. If a child of five years' actual age can do everything that the average child of that age can do, his mental age is also five years. But if he is a very intelligent child, he may be able to do what the average child of seven can do. Then we say he has a *mental* age of seven. If, however, he can achieve only what the average child of four can do, then his mental age is four even though his birthday age is five.

Gesell applies this concept to the infants and younger children whom he studies, too. Having discovered the average skill and understanding of children during the successive months and years—two months, six months, twelve months, two years, and so on, he can then compare the mental level of any given child with the norm, and express the child's development in terms of his mental age. Thus a highly intelligent or " precocious " two-year-old may behave like an ordinary child of two and a half, but a backward two-year-old may have a mental age only of, say, twenty-one or even eighteen months.

Now one of the first things that is established when development is studied in this way is that there is no necessary relation between " precocity " and nervousness. Many intelligent children are nervous, but that is not a result of their intelligence. Many ordinary or dull children are " highly strung " too ; and a great many exceptionally intelligent children are stable and healthy. The " nervousness " is a function of other conditions, either within the child's emotional life or outside in the environment—or both.

**Heredity and education.** Another most important conclusion, supported by all studies of the development of intelligence, is that it is extremely probable that the level of general ability which a child shows in his earliest years will be maintained throughout his later life. In saying this, however, we distinguish sharply between the child's inborn abilities and the actual use which is made of these native gifts by the education we provide for him. Our intelligence does appear to be mainly

born in us, not acquired ; but the use we make of it is
mostly decided by the education we enjoy.

It is not, however, suggested that a young child will
not improve his comparative level in any of the details
of his early manipulative skill or speech.  He may go
either up or down in any of these details.  He may start
slowly and catch up later, or start well and slow down
a little, in any single sort of performance, or even several
sorts.  When we say he is not likely to change his general
level of ability to any marked degree, we mean his general
level as shown by the pooled results of his total behaviour
at any given age.  And even this statement cannot yet
be made of infants and very young children as studied
by Gesell's or other tests, with the same sureness that
it can be made of children over five as studied by the
Binet tests.  The time may come when we can diagnose
the comparative intelligence of infants and small children
as reliably as we now can that of eight- and ten-year-
olds ; but it is not yet.  Gesell is able to show us steady
curves of development in gifted or backward children
even from the earliest months, keeping consistently
above or below the average, but much remains to be
done in the way of general confirmation of these results
and of the detailed tests on which they are based.

The general conclusion that intelligence is mainly a
function of heredity rather than of environment is however well established, and has a significance reaching far
beyond the purpose of this volume.  Here I can neither
give the evidence for the view nor hint at its social
importance.  But its everyday bearings for practical
parents may be brought out a little further.

It may at first sight seem a discouraging conclusion
to parents who are anxious to do everything they can for

their children ; but in fact it is not so.  For whatever we have already given our children in giving them life, it still remains true that they can only realise their highest potentialities of mental growth if we give them also the best conditions of play and work.  The intelligent child can only reap the fruit of his intelligence if he has what his mind needs to work upon.  The duller child needs to be helped too, to ensure that none even of his lesser gifts shall be wasted.  Wherever inheritance ends, education has still to begin.

**Gifted children.**  And if we are fortunate in having gifted children, how good to know that we need not fear their " precocity ".  A child who can do and think in the way natural to the average child of older years is simply a more intelligent child.  We need not worry that his greater intelligence will die away later on, nor that it means nervous instability or ill-health.  It need not in the least mean this, provided only we refrain from pushing him on, and let him go his own pace.  He needs as many opportunities for active play and a healthy physical life as his duller friends.  Given these, we can safely take pleasure in his intelligence and let him have the appropriate means to feed it.

There is thus no basis for the idea that we must " keep back " the intelligent child.  If we try to do that either in school or home, we make him restless and mischievous, or baffled and miserable.  There are only too many bright young children whose impulses of mental growth are starved or obstructed in the nursery by the idea that they must not be too " forward ".  They are not allowed to ask intelligent questions about the world, or are laughed at if they do.  They are not given the chance to fend for themselves, nor to develop all the gifts of creative expression and understanding that are surging in them.

While, then, we can use our knowledge of what average children are able to do at given ages to keep our *demands* upon children's behaviour reasonable and sane, we need not try to make all our children alike nor keep them all at the same dead level of skill and independence.

**Backward children.** Some knowledge of age-norms is also very useful for those who have relatively backward children. It would always be desirable for a parent of a backward child to have the causes of this condition inquired into as early as possible, and if the parent can tell that the child is not up to the normal mental level for his age, he is more likely to seek expert advice. Only the highly trained psychologist can make an *exact* estimate of the level of a child's intelligence. The ordinary parent cannot do that, and it would be a mistake for him to imagine he could. But he might use his general knowledge of age-norms to gain some idea as to whether the child is ahead or backward of the usual child of his age, and if need shows, can then turn to those who know how to inquire into the actual sources of the backwardness.

If it should turn out that the causes are not in circumstances that can be altered, as does very often appear with backward children, then at least the parent will be spared later years of unnecessary self-reproach. If they lie in conditions that can be remedied—emotional inhibitions open to psychological treatment, methods of training or living—then the earlier they are seen to, the better.

**Backwardness in speech.** There is one particular direction in which this is specially true, that of speech development. I have already quoted Gesell's norms for twelve to twenty-four months. Individual children however differ a good deal in the age at which they begin to use words clearly and intelligibly. Even within the range of normality, there are big differences. It is not at all uncommon, for instance, to find an intelligent boy of two years who does not speak at all, although it seems clear from his facial expression and general behaviour that he understands most of what is said to him. (Boys are on the average a month or so later than girls.) One thus does not need to worry about his not beginning to speak at this age. He is quite likely to begin with clear words and well-formed sentences soon after he is two.

But if he does not begin by the time he is three, then some inquiry should be made into the causes of this late development. That is important because language itself is so important. Words are essential tools of thinking, and without them the child's understanding will inevitably be handicapped. Think of the passion of the ordinary child for naming things, and his delight in new words and phrases ! Much is going to be lost to the child who has not this fine instrument of knowledge and communication—much both of understanding and of social experience. Hence we should not delay to discover the reason for the hold-up, and to remedy it if it can be remedied.

The possible causes are of at least four sorts. There may be (a) An all-round defect of intelligence, itself irremediable. (b) An all-round inhibition of the emotional life, of the kind that might later appear as a serious disturbance of the mental life as a whole. This a few psychologists are now beginning to understand

and to deal with.  (c) A less serious emotional inhibition, due perhaps to intense rivalry with an older child of the family, who is himself perhaps clever and gifted in speech. In such a case a change of environment—separation from the older child, a nursery school and skilled and sympathetic handling, may relieve the trouble.  (d) A localised defect of the speech mechanisms, either organic or psychological, which may possibly be relieved by skilled treatment and training.

In any of these cases but the first, the difficulty can often be lessened or removed ; but the chances of benefit are the greater the earlier the problem is attacked.

**Need for research.** I have now indicated a few of the practical uses to which our growing knowledge of age-norms of development can be put. There are, besides, many important scientific problems which can only be tackled on the basis of a more exact understanding of these age-norms, and which in their turn may have practical bearings. One example is the question of the influence of glandular deficiencies and glandular treatment upon the growth of intelligence. We already know that one form of mental defect, cretinism, is due to thyroid deficiency, and can be greatly relieved by continued thyroid treatment. There are probably many interesting and significant discoveries of this sort still to be made.

Much research is yet needed, however, not only on such problems, but directly on the norms of development themselves. There are many things still to be studied about the growth of skill and the development of speech. The norms I have already quoted are tentative and may still have to be revised ; and they certainly need further revision for English children.   Parents could, in fact, here be of the greatest assistance to psychological and educational science, by keeping exact and full records of the development of their own children in all these respects.

## CHAPTER V

## TWO TO SIX: THE CHILD AND THE WORLD

DEVELOPMENT of skills. Turning now to children who can walk and talk, we see them practising and perfecting their bodily skills with more zest than ever. Walking and running, jumping and climbing, throwing and balancing, threading beads and drawing—each is tried and attained in its turn. We don't have to teach children to do these things. They do them, with passion and delight, if we leave them room and opportunity. We can hinder them by saying " don't ", and " sit still " ; by asking the wrong things of them, and giving them the wrong things to play with—to " sew a fine seam ", for example, or to do fine writing at a time when their muscles need large things to hold and large sweeping movement. On the other hand, by studying the ways of their growth, we can give them things to do and to play with which will feed their skill and power.

It is very important to know that the larger movements ripen first, and the finer skills only much later— hip and shoulder and knee before wrist and ankle ; the coarser movements of the hand as a whole before the finer combinations of the fingers. To give children things to use or ask them to do things which reverse this order is to make them tired and bad-tempered. All this might seem obvious ; but it is still often forgotten or over-looked in buying bricks and writing or sewing material for young children, and in setting our general standard of what they should be able to do.

**Value of movement.** Moreover, the restless general movement of little children, so trying in grown-ups in the railway carriage, or even in the home, is itself an impulse of growth. To sit still is the most difficult thing for the little child—and to sit still for long would be the worst thing he could do. For he grows and becomes skilful only by moving and doing. He learns to run by running ; to balance and carry by trying to balance and carry. His mistakes and clumsinesses are necessary milestones on the path to skill and poise, and the doing and trying are more important than the mistakes of the moment. If John falls down when running and makes his knees dirty, or Mary drops the cup of water she is carrying, it is well to remember that these events, however inconvenient to us, are incidents in learning to run easily and quickly, or learning to carry and balance skilfully. Scoldings may only increase the clumsiness, and further practice with friendly encouragement is all that is needed—although to ask John to help make his knees clean again, and Mary to wipe up the water she spilt, may lead to greater care.

The study of young children's muscular development, and their impulses to movement, have shown that these latter can on the whole be trusted. (So, for that matter, can their occasional desire to do nothing at all.) Children's pleasure in climbing and holding on by their arms, or swinging, and their rebellion against standing in a row " toeing the line "—all these are the natural outcome of the fact that the bones of the legs are still soft and unable to support the weight of the relatively large trunk and head, steadily and continuously. Nor can children in these early years keep their balance when standing still for more than a short time, without undue strain. They love, however, to practise keeping their balance when moving—walking along the top of a wall, the edge of the pavement, or a chalk line on the floor. And to try to sit perfectly still for an occasional *short* time is a great game, as Dr. Montessori has taught us.

In general, our aim should be to give children as many opportunities of free movement as possible, and to make use for social purposes of their love of doing things. Helping to lay and clear the meal table, to carry jugs and cups, to dress and undress themselves, to hang up their own clothes and wash their own hands—all these are things that little children may delight in, and that help their control and balance as well as their independence. If these are suggested, not as tasks they ought to do for moral reasons, but as games which they may share with us, little children take pride and pleasure in doing them, even though the spoons are not at first laid quite so straight, nor the coat hung up quite so tidily as it might be.

**Curiosity and interest in events.** Another very important fact about healthy children, from the time they begin to walk, is their lively curiosity about everything that goes on around them. Their eager senses and intelligence reach out for forms and colours, sounds and surfaces, just as their bodies for food. Walking and running are enjoyed not only for the pleasure of actual movement, but also for the new discoveries of space they bring. For the knowledge of space relations grows by the fusion of what is seen and touched with the feelings of one's own movements in stretching or walking through the space seen. At the later time when questions begin, this space interest takes the form of queries about " how far ? " and " how big ? " and the delight in measuring and comparing the sizes of things. At first again only large differences in size and distance can be appreciated ; then the finer ones.

After they have gained some mastery of space relations and of their movements in walking, children become actively interested in the things and events of the home and the street. Everything that we take as a matter of course may be full of keen interest to them. The cooking and cleaning in the kitchen, washing and bathing, finding out where the water in the lavatory pipes goes to and comes from, lighting a candle and turning gas-taps, switching the electric light on and off, trying to see what things will burn and what won't, noticing the bodily processes of eating and drinking and excreting, observing the rain and the sun, watching trains and trams—this is the kind of thing upon which children's minds are at work all the time, observing and comparing, remembering and judging and reasoning. We know how many and how constant are the questions poured out in these early years—" How does the water get up into the pipes ? Why does water spread out flat—why won't it stay up in the middle ? Where does the sky end ? How small will you be when I am grown-up ? Why are there stones in the ground ? How can the hippo get down the steps into his tank when his little front legs are such a long way off his little back legs ? *Why* don't you know ? " And so on, without end.[1] And if the grown-up should be too busy or too impatient to attend, the child (of, e.g., four years) may protest, " Oh, Mummy ! You're no good at questions this morning."

" **Don't touch.**" Along with the questions goes the impulse to pull things to pieces—clocks and engines ; to open boxes and drawers, to explore cupboards and tunnels, to " see wheels go round ". Children *learn* by their fingers—without active touch their vision as yet tells them little ; and without their actual sensory experience of things, what other people tell them means hardly anything at all. There could not be a more cruel or a more stupid thing said to little children than " don't touch ". It simply means " don't learn, don't grow, don't be intelligent ". As the babe at the breast thinks with his mouth, so children of older years think with their fingers and limbs. Very slowly does the power to think with words develop—much more slowly than it may seem to those of us who are misled by children's imitative ways in speech. It is easy, for instance, to get children to repeat glibly " twice five are ten ", long before they understand this number relation. In the schools, we have realised this, and altered our methods of teaching accordingly. But even some professional educators do not yet recognise how easy it is to mistake words for knowledge, and how much more vivid and usable is the understanding which children get from immediate experience of doing things, and finding out for themselves, than from being told about them.

[1] For a psychological study of the meaning of some of these questions, see the Appendix on " Children's ' Why ' Questions," by Nathan Isaacs, in my *Intellectual Growth in Young Children.*

Words are at first merely a way of pointing to things, and but empty sounds until the children have had a rich contact with the things themselves, and explored them with hand and eye. It is by walking and stretching and touching that the words " far " and " near ", " large " and " small ", gain their meaning. It is by actually seeing the " wheels go round ", by lifting and pushing and pulling, by taking things apart and fitting them together, by measuring and weighing, that children gain their knowledge of physical changes and properties—not by having these things " explained " to them. To find out for oneself, to watch and repeat and watch again, for example, the way water makes a channel for itself through sand, the way one's toy boat turns over when caught in the swift current of the stream, or the way one moves faster or slower if one has a sliding board inclined more steeply or less—these are the experiences which give reality to the later study of " physics " and " mechanics ", in which we shall want our children to be interested and to do well.

" Let's find out." Our descriptions and explanations are useful when children are older, to supplement their own experience ; but they are useless as a substitute for it. *We* may like explaining, but it is not always the most useful thing for our children. Whatever they can discover by their own efforts in exploring and experimenting, they should. And our general aim should be to encourage them to find out as much as possible for themselves, turning to us for help or information really beyond their own reach. Our best reply to many of their questions would often be " What do you think ? " " Shall we try ? " " Let's find out "—

rather than " It *is* so-and-so ". For if we indulge in the habit of giving information dogmatically every time, the children get into the corresponding habit of asking for it—sometimes because they want to please us, sometimes because our way of being all-wise has made them helpless.

**Destructiveness.** No less eager than their desire to explore the world is the pleasure of little children in making things—and, sometimes, in destroying them! Children just beginning to walk often delight more, for a time, in knocking down the towers of bricks built by elder brothers, than in piling them up for themselves. The quick explosive movement of knocking down is, of course, much easier than the effort of building up, and needs less attention and less control. It is thus a definite relief of nervous tension ; and is, indeed, not without its pleasure and emotional value for older children. A certain amount of destructiveness is quite normal in these years, particularly with boys. Ways can be found of making use of such explosive action, for example, in chopping up wood, burning rubbish on the garden bonfire, or tearing and cutting up paper to make coloured streamers or to stuff a doll's pillow. And it is important to make sure that the destructive child has ample free exercise, particularly of the larger joints, in the open air—in running, and throwing, jumping and climbing.

**Making things.** As their skill and control develop, however, children's delight in making and inventing things, with every sort of material coming to their hands, is unceasing. Anything and everything is pressed into service, according to the purpose of the moment and the skill of the children. Hands cannot be inactive nor imagination infertile, as long as children are free to make and do. Again, what pleasure and interest parents lose for themselves, as well as for their children, if they fail to meet this passionate urge for making and doing ; and if, instead of providing things to use and room to use them in, they try to force this productive stream of energy into the negative channels of " sitting still " or " keeping your clothes clean ". Sometimes we do seem thoughtlessly to give more weight to merely formal manners than to growth in constructive power and the self-respect which real achievement brings. Yet the manners which can be trusted to work well when we are not there to enforce them grow only out of a happy free friendliness to grown-ups, which is in its turn the fruit of the child's experience of his parents' friendliness and understanding of his needs.

**Room and furniture.** As a practical outcome of these facts, then, we should give our children as much room in house and garden, for free movement and for making and doing, as we possibly can. In any ordinary household, there are, of course, physical limits to what we can do in this way ; but if we remember that room for running and climbing and balancing, and for creative play, is a real necessity of children's growth, we shall not put the tidiness and symmetry of our rooms or the perfection of our gardens before their health and happiness ; and may even be willing to curtail our own space rather than theirs.

Then, also, if children's pleasure in doing things for themselves is to be made use of, they need tables and chairs of the right size, shelves for their crockery, sponge and washing bowl, cupboards for their toys, hooks for their clothes, all at the right height. They need plenty of playthings (of which I shall speak later), and some place of their own to keep these in ; and ample floor-space for their various floor-games. We can reasonably ask them not to spoil our possessions —our furniture and books and tended garden—only if we leave them free to have their own things, and respect these as scrupulously as we ask them to respect ours.

Should we, if we have the space to spare, give the children a whole day-room to themselves ? And should we then keep them to it ? The great advantage of the " day nursery ", as of the Nursery School, is that it can be specially fitted and arranged to suit the children's size and skill ; and that their playthings need not be put away just for the convenience of elders. There is nothing more tantalising for children than to have to interrupt or spoil a modelled railway or farm, or other floor-game, or even an imaginative arrangement of chairs and tables, just because it is dinner-time or bedtime. Given the chance, they will often carry on the things they have made, developing them from day to day, for weeks at a time—and nothing could be a more valuable training in patience and sustained effort. So important are these two considerations that the parent in the smaller home, who has not a room obviously to spare, may nevertheless be willing to put himself out a good deal to secure these solid advantages for his children. It would be worth while, for example, to give up the separate formal dining-room, if that meant that they could have it as a play and workroom during the daytime at least ; or, at a pinch, one end of it, with the children's own cupboard. And if we

can give them a corner of the garden to be their very
own, where they are free to put what things they
please, and to dig up the seeds and bulbs to see if they
are growing as often as they like, and to learn that
they will not grow that way—will not this, besides
giving them the chance to find out all sorts of things
about soil and plants and weather, also make it easier
for them not to pluck our lilies or run over our rose-
beds ?

**The nursery and the kitchen.** Where children can
have a room entirely of their own, however, they should
nevertheless not be confined to it. The room should
be made for them, and not they for the room. In
itself, it cannot provide enough stimulus for active
minds. Children need also to watch mother or cook
in the kitchen, and to try to do the things done there,
to be with her when she shops or sews or gardens.
These things give the child a living sense of companionship with adults, and call out his intelligence, no less
than the playthings specially made for the particular
stage of active understanding and of manual skill which
he has reached. He needs both kinds of experience—
real achievement of his own, which can only come if
he has play material and real things to use of the right
sort and size ; and the sharing of what grown-ups do,
by observation and imaginative play.

This latter means, however, that we have to be ready
to share *his* interests in these things, and not to feel
his questions and his efforts to do what we are doing
as just an interference with our serious pursuits. We
have to be interested with him in finding out about
the way the bath-water runs down the pipes, or what
happens to the cake if we put more or less milk into

it, or cook it for a shorter or longer time ; in counting the houses in our street, in adding up the change we get at the shop, in watching the trains at the station, and finding out about the signals and shunting. If we share his eager interest in these things, and feel our way into his ponderings about them, how different, for example, our walks and excursions with him become. No longer do we want to make him walk quietly and dully, beside us, compelling his legs, which left to themselves would leap and run and skip even on the public highway, to plod one step after another, in the stolid way of the adult—a thing infinitely harder and less useful for the growing child. No longer do we want to make his mind sober and pedestrian and prematurely ordered, if we can once come to see the delight of his keen questionings about everything as he goes about the world.

CHAPTER VI

## TWO TO SIX: THE CHILD AND HIS PARENTS

**P**RIMITIVE **feelings.** In the last chapter, we talked chiefly of little children's interest in things. But we cannot be too clear that at this stage all the world of things that *we* live in is only beginning to come into the mental life of the child. Most of this world—almost all that goes to make up our sense of proportion and values—is thus still lacking. But the child's human relations are there, and immensely important for him, from the start. And his feelings about them must long retain their primitive form and force, just because there is so little yet to compete with them or to limit them. That can only come through all the gradual ways of the child's growth. Meanwhile, however, he expresses and acts out these rudimentary feelings in countless revealing ways. We can only describe them by the nearest analogies in our world, but we cannot hope to understand them unless we first imagine away everything that the young child still lacks, and then see these primary feelings as all the more real and powerful for that.

**The babe's love.** We have seen how the babe at the breast is able to feel again one with his mother, as if he had her as entirely his own. But the fact that his wants are not always satisfied at once, his mother coming

80

and going according to her own will and wisdom rather than his imperious wishes, leads him slowly to see her as herself a person, with her own life and her own desires and interests—not just as a breast to feed him and arms to serve him. The child, however, goes on wanting the loved person altogether to himself. And in these early years, love means for children the full-bodied sensory pleasure of caresses. Only slowly does it grow beyond this, and come to mean also the non-sensual pleasures of mutual devotion and service, talk and common interests. So the father's love, too, means to the very little child the intense pleasure of being lifted in his firm strong arms, and caressed with loving hands and voice.

We have already noted the importance of the mouth, and presently of the anus, as centres of sensual pleasure in these earliest days. Even towards the end of the first year, however, it is to be seen that the genital organs also begin to play their part. This is true of both boy and girl, although it is more easily observed in the boy, whose organ tends to become erect when he is fed or caressed or feeling affectionate, and is some-times fingered by the infant himself. The excitement of the genitals by any sort of caress or the feeling of affection goes on all through these early years, and is again a normal fact. At this time, children have not yet become free of this deepest bodily core in any of their affections. Sensual pleasure has not yet been canalised into the definite path of mature sexual love, as it will be in the later years of growth, but is still intimately connected with all affections and attachments.

**Frustration and anger.** About the time when he begins to walk and talk, the child has more or less come to know both father and mother as persons, with lives and wills of their own, and to love them *as* other persons. But it is not a simple unalloyed love he feels, and cannot be. The very separateness of the mother brings frustration and anger ; the independent coming and going of the father inevitably means some failure to meet all the child's wishes. We saw in the chapter on infancy how this anger and sense of frustration is often expressed by biting the breast or other people's fingers.

As the children grow and move about, the ways in which they come into conflict with the wishes of the parents, and the parents' with theirs, increase likewise. How slowly any appreciation of the point of view of other persons develops is illustrated in the argument of a boy in his fourth year, which might well be called " the philosophy of ' I want ' ". When the grown-ups refused to pick up something he had thrown from his pram, he insisted, " But I want them to ! " " Why ? " " Because I like it." " But they don't like it." " But they *must !* " " Why must they, if they don't like it ? " " Because I want them to ! "

These clashes inevitably call out disappointment, rage and defiance in the child, as was vividly shown in Scupin's description of the thwarted infant already quoted. And the nature of rage, in which there is always something blind, is to push away and destroy the obstacle to desire—even if it be the person whom at other moments the child loves.

The younger child shows his rage by cries and gestures, defiance with his bowel, attempts to bite or hit, a passionate refusal of food. The older can to some extent voice his feelings in words as well as in acts. But since we usually check any manifestations of rage in their very beginning, few children beyond the first year of infancy give full expression to the strength of their anger and defiance. If they are not too afraid of us, they may say, " You horrid, unkind thing ". Or, as a child of five said resentfully to her mother after being scolded for cutting her hair, " If you would go away altogether, I could do my hair as I liked ! "

It has, however, been found by those who have observed children under conditions planned to reveal more of what their feelings really are, that when words are not checked children express their rage and defiance vividly and intensely. They will say to any adults or other children who interfere with their wishes, no matter how devoted they may be at other times, " You beast ! I hate you ! " " I'll kill you ! " This " hate " of the child does not mean the settled disposition which we should mean by hate. It is both more intense and more momentary ; but it is the source from which the settled disposition of hate may grow if the rage-impulses become attached to any person who habitually calls them out.

We can greatly increase the child's hate and give it a hold over him by despotism or lack of thought and understanding ; or we can lessen it by patient friendliness and steady love. But we cannot rule it out altogether. The best-cared-for and happiest child will have his moments of anger, defiance and destructiveness. Even if he hides them from us because they would displease us, they will be there underneath. And without some impulses to turn away from us, how would he leave behind his infant's way of clinging to his parents ? How come to feel himself as an independent person, free to turn to the social world and stand on his own feet as an adult ?

**Jealousy and rivalry.** Moreover, as early as the end of the first year, children come also to feel conflict between love for their father and love for their mother. It is no easier for them to love both at once and equally than it is for adults to keep an even attachment between three close friends, or to prevent the tension of rivalry between two men and a woman, or two women and a man. Indeed, it is far more difficult for the child, because of the intensity of his desires and his complete dependence upon his parents. When he loves his mother, he wants her all to himself ; and when he is enjoying the presence and caresses of his father, the entry of his mother disturbs the balance again.

Very early the preference of most little boys for the caresses of their mothers can be seen, and the greater delight of the little girl in her father. Occasionally, however, the reverse picture can be made out quite early ; and in any case there is rarely a simple clear preference for the one and distaste or indifference to the other. The little boy admires and loves his father for his strength and size and skill and wisdom. He wants to be like him, and tries in his imitative play to do the wonderful things father does. And yet he comes to fear and hate him because of his claim to the mother's love, which the boy, in his infantile absoluteness, wants to have all to himself. " It's best when we're alone, mummy, isn't it ? " as one boy said.

The little girl, too, typically wants to have her father all to herself. She may love and admire her mother, and want to be like her. But she also wants to take her mother's place with the father, and have his gift of children for herself. " When I'm a grown-up lady. I'm going to marry Daddy." " And what will your

Mummy do then ? " " Oh, she'll be a little baby then."

This possessive devotion to the father is often shifted on to men friends. One little girl of five years invited a man friend of the family to come and stay at her house with her. He replied that there was not a room free for him, as was true. " Oh, but you can sleep with me—I should like to have three—you and me and my dolly ! "

Very often this rivalry makes the little girl afraid of her mother. She may then try to keep her fear at bay by open challenge and defiance, often alternating with moments of penitent and even passionate affection— " Oh, Mummy, I do, *do* love you ! " And with some girl children the whole situation of rivalry and wish for the father is successfully covered up by the greatest devotion to the wishes of the mother, which may even last on into later life.

**Jealousy of younger children.** The birth of a younger child may intensify this situation acutely. To the child who is displaced from his mother's lap by the newcomer, it seems that now there is a second rival to her attention and love. He is puzzled to know why he has been displaced ; and, since it seems that the new helpless baby gains her care by his helplessness, he will often return to his own babyishness, as a possible way of regaining attention. He will now again want to be fed on her lap, complain more often that he is tired and wants to be carried, cry more easily, or show less control over his bladder and bowels, than for some time previously.

" Since the new baby came, Jane (aged 22 months) seems to whine and cry if things are not just to her liking, and if I take her into the drawing-room to see visitors, we have quite an outburst—she clutches me tight and sobs.  She was some days before she would go near the new baby, but now she is very interested and does not seem jealous." [1]  Instead of the open jealousy, Jane shows this querulousness and fear of strangers.

"My little boy is one year and ten months old, and his sister is nine months.  He was very unhappy at her arrival and used to try and pull her off my lap.  Now he is on the whole very good to her—tries to protect her from ' bumps ', shares things with her, and so on. But if he is tired and hurts himself, at once he wants my exclusive attention.  And now he has a funny new trick.  If anything goes wrong, or at the slightest word of censure, he flops down and *crawls*.  He has walked since he was ten months old, and is particularly active and sure-footed—can run and climb like a three-year-old.  He is generally very independent, quite clean night and day, feeds himself tidily.  But now he crawls in this way.  This is, I suppose, because when the baby crawls we admire and praise her, and so he wants admiration too."

But open displays of angry jealousy and threats to the little intruder are by no means uncommon.

"My little boy of three-and-a-half has now for some time been so unkind to his little sister of thirteen months. To give you an example :  he rushed into the nursery yesterday to tell me about something he was doing, and seeing the baby on my lap, he smacked her three times across the face.  After the first smack, I said,

---

[1] This and some of my other illustrations are from problems put to me by parents.

' How unkind—why do you do that ? ' But before I could stop him he had done it again twice. He will also hit her when I am not in the room."

And the intensity of the child's jealousy may affect not only behaviour, but even health. A striking instance of this came my way recently, that of a little girl of two and a half, a bright intelligent child, developing normally in body and mind. As there was no prospect of brothers and sisters, and no playmates near at hand, the mother arranged for another little girl (fourteen months older) and her mother, to join the household. They came, and for a few weeks everything went splendidly. The two children played together most happily, to the delight of both mothers. The little one whose home it was seemed to look upon the other as a temporary guest whose presence she enjoyed. Then, apparently, she began to realise that this was no guest, here to-day and gone to-morrow—but a permanent intruder into the home where hitherto she herself had reigned supreme ! She became terribly jealous and miserable, screaming with jealous rage all day long. This lasted for some weeks, and her weight chart in this period shows the effect of this mental strain upon her bodily health in the most striking way. The figures run : October 16, 28 lb. 12 oz. ; October 23, 28 lb. 15 oz. ; October 30, 29 lb. ; November 6, 29 lb. 1 oz. ; November 13, 29 lb. 8 oz. ; November 20, 30 lb. 3 oz. So far, a steady gain, as normally. Then comes the period of tears and misery, and the weight goes *down*. November 27, 29 lb. 12 oz. ; December 4, 29 lb. 9 oz. After this, the increase begins again, but goes very slowly and fitfully ; December 11, 29 lb. 10 oz. ; December 18, 30 lb. 1 oz. ; January 1, 30 lb. 3 oz. ; January 8, 30 lb. 2 oz. And then normal growth was resumed, as the child came to accept the social situation rather more cheerfully. Later on, the children were most excellent playmates. Fortunately, both mothers were very sensible and patient in handling the difficulty when it was at its most trying, and in the end the little hostess undoubtedly benefited in all-round development from the companionship of the other child. But the weight chart was a very interesting demonstration of the way in which bodily growth can be affected by purely mental causes. There was nothing to account for the drop in weight but the emotional disturbance, since there was no other change in circumstances.

We can, indeed, safely say that *all* children feel such jealousy of the new arrival in their home, although some *show* it more plainly than others. The child is jealous chiefly because of his dread that mother or nurse no longer loves him. He fears they love the newcomer better than him. Many children even (and this is the worst thing of all) come to feel that if they had themselves been really good and loving children all the time, mother would never have *wanted* any more ! The new baby is to them a proof that they did not please mother enough in their behaviour ; and thus they feel quite sure that she must love the baby better than she does them. That is why this jealousy is sometimes so overpowering, and why the little child needs all our help to get over it. And the only way we can help him is by making quite plain that we do love him just as much, and that we are always equally just and equally loving to all. It is not enough to take this for granted in our own minds. We need to show it in ways the child himself can understand.

**Mothering the new baby.** The intelligent child who

has already reached some degree of self-control and is by nature very loving can, however, be very quick in hiding his feelings from those whom they will displease. And some children very early indeed adapt to the new situation by ranging themselves on the side of the parents, behaving as if they were the parents, being generous and protective to the new baby, and so turning the edge of their jealousy and of the feeling of inferiority which the coming of the new baby meant for them. A little girl of three, for example, usually independent, cheerful and full of fun, in whose home twins arrived, showed for a time a marked return to babyish ways— wanting to be carried, crying at the least denial, getting easily tired and irritable, and unable to do anything for herself, for some weeks after the event. But presently she told visitors, " I've got twins ", and took over the mother's rôle of tender care and interest for them—and slowly regained her normal self-confidence and balance. By being the mother to them, she was again able to feel superior to them, and so to love them.

This is the sort of adaptation which pleases most of us, and the one perhaps to be in the end desired. Yet we have to remember that whilst it is a pleasant solution for us, it is only achieved in the child by great effort. We must not be surprised to find that along with it goes a general increase in " nervousness " and readiness for fatigue. The child's successful covering up of her troubles must not deceive us into believing that she has none ; nor must we blame and scold those children who cannot so readily put a fair face on things, and who are more obviously given up to primitive rivalries and distresses. Given time, and our cheerful patience, they also may come to accept the fact of the new baby, and may possibly do so far more securely and at a smaller price of nervous energy than the child who has attempted it too early. At least, we may remember that all children do suffer these pangs, and must, from the facts of their own nature. From whence would spring all our adult rivalries for love and place and power, in the sexual relation, in family life, in politics, business and social affairs, if they had not their roots in these first personal tensions ?

**The only child.** Nor, as we have seen, does it need an actual birth in the child's own family to call out fear of being displaced. One of the most intense and open jealousies I have observed in a four-year-old child was in the case of an only boy, who, on being taken to join a group of other little children, could not make friends with any of them. He pushed them down and pinched them, and tried to keep the attention of every friendly grown-up to himself ; and presently confided to one of the latter, " It's better for me when there aren't any other children about, isn't it ? "

It is, of course, widely recognised that the only child, who never has any brothers and sisters, is liable to special difficulties of behaviour and typical faults of character. If then the birth of a younger child seems to bring about an emotional disturbance, how comes it that the only child is not better off ? The full answer to this most interesting problem would take us deeper into the psychology of little children than we have room to go, but, briefly, it is in the main for the following reasons :

In the first place, fears of possible rivals are active in all children from an early age. They arise in part from the child's earliest rivalries and hostilities in regard to the parents, and from phantasies of loss of the mother's love or punishment from the father's anger. Such fears are strengthened by the child's occasional contacts with visiting children or with new babies in other homes.

Now when the dreaded thing happens, and a younger child is born to his own parents, it seems for a time as if the very worst had come true. But if his parents handle the older child sensibly and lovingly, then he finds that after all his world has not in fact been turned completely topsy-turvy or destroyed because other children have come. His parents *do* still love him, and his worst and most secret fears turn out (provided his parents do not exploit his jealousies) to have little or no foundation in reality. And so they lose much of their hold upon him.

The only child, however, whilst he does not suffer the actual crisis of the real event, never gains the great comfort and support of real experience. His phantasies of loss and punishment are never dispersed by the steady light of reality. They are thus able to retain a far deeper hold, making him petulant and hostile to strangers and tyrannical with his mother.

Secondly, the actual monopoly of his parents which the only child enjoys keeps his appetite for possession inordinate, and makes him quite unable to tolerate the least denial of his demands.

In the third place, the child who is fortunate enough to have real brothers and sisters finds in them splendid allies against the world of the grown-ups. They understand his world of values as no adult can ever do. The only child is alone against the all-knowing and all-powerful grown-ups. The family of children finds comradeship in play, and their common weakness becomes strength.

And finally, on the basis of this comradeship, the family of brothers and sisters educate each other by the give-and-take of actual social life. This real education by social experience is altogether missed by the only child.

The hopes and fears of the early rivalry may, nevertheless, linger on even in those older children who have adapted most successfully to the presence of the younger ; as with the boy of six, who was on excellent terms of elder-brotherhood with his brother of four and a half, but, nevertheless, asked his mother wistfully one day, " Mummy, which do you like best—me or David ? "

(Whilst David himself, the younger brother, illustrates for us the problem of the younger child, with which there is no space to deal here. David overcomes his own rivalry by a great pride in being the brother of such a wonderful person. One day, when his father was admiringly watching David turning somersaults, David said, " Yes, you know, I'm the second cleverest person in the world—no, I'm the *third*—Jack is the first *and* second cleverest ! " But he gave the obverse of this picture another day, by saying to his mother, " Mummy, Jack's older than me, isn't he ? " " Yes." " Then he'll die first, won't he ? ")

" Where do babies come from ? " Thus are little children in these critical early years torn and tossed between their loves and their hates, between the delights of possession and the fears and anxieties of loss. And it is these fears and anxieties that lie behind their questions as to " where babies come from ".

Such questions do not arise in the little child's mind from mere idle curiosity, nor from a pure desire for knowledge as such. They spring from deep ponderings about his own relationship to his parents and his brothers and sisters ; from his fear of rivals, actual or possible and from a groping and searching after some meaning in what he dimly senses of his own history and growth, his own past and future. He sees around him men and women, old and young, big children and little. He sees new babies arrive or hears of them in other families. Where did they come from ? How did they begin ? Will they grow up too ? What *is* growing up ? What is " having " a baby ? What does it feel like ?

How strange it would be if an intelligent observant child did not ask questions about the drama of human life in this way ! He would have to be blind and deaf and stupid not to do so. Or (as alas ! does happen only too often) to be locked up in solitary and fruitless musings by shyness and fear.

**The wish for a baby.** Lying behind these questions are many others, rising from the depths of his hopes and fears. He wonders inarticulately why he is excluded from the special privileges of love between the father and mother, which he vaguely senses ; and seeing the pride and pleasure of the parents in the new babe, he longs himself to produce so wonderful an evidence of love and power. " Shall *I* have a baby when I'm grown up ? " both boys and girls ask.

The little girl may show her wish for babies more openly and unconcernedly in speech or play with dolls. But the boy often has this secret wish too, even where the grown-ups subtly succeed in making him hide it. He may show it naïvely in a sympathetic atmosphere. A boy of four recently said to his mother a day or two after the cat had had kittens : " Mummy, I'm growing

a baby sister ! " " Oh, no, John, you can't—only
mummies can do that ! " " Well, then it's a baby
brother ! " " Oh, no, my dear, you can't grow a baby.
Only mummies can do that." " Well, Mummy,
*something's* happening in my tummy ! "

**The age of questions.** The open question as to
where babies come from may arise, if children are not
too frightened to ask, at any time from the fourth year
onwards. A very intelligent child may arrive at it even
at three years of age, although commonly it comes a
little later. " My little boy of three is beginning to ask
questions which are difficult to answer. He has asked
me several times where he came from ; before that he
used to ask who looked after him when I was little and
had to go to school."

And sometimes a child whose emotional development
is unusually satisfactory, so that his intelligence moves
unhampered, may solve the problem happily for himself. " We don't know any families where there is a
baby, so there was no definite reason for his opinion.
Mark (aged four and a half) was looking at a book,
showing a picture of a hen and some eggs. He said
' The mummy hen laid those eggs ', and then went on
to all the animals he could remember as laying eggs.
Then he suddenly realised that many animals don't,
and said ' Mummy horses lay baby horses ', and so on.
Then, ' Well, Mummy must have laid me ! ' Mark was
talking to himself, and said nothing further to me (his
Mummy) or nurse at the time."

**Jealousy and guilt.** Such a happy outcome of the
child's deep ponderings on his own origins is, however,
not as common as we might wish. In the case of some
children, indeed, their thoughts are so strongly charged

with emotion that they cannot even express them, let alone ask the direct question, " Where do babies come from ? " And so their parents fondly imagine that they " never think about such things " !

Yet the emotional conflict from which these wonderings arise is there in all children. Some show the stress of their voiceless anxiety even to unobservant eyes. Others are better able to keep a cheerful front, and to adapt more quickly to their recognition that we should not be pleased to see their jealousies and angers and dislikes. But the further our study of the emotional life of little children is carried, the more clearly do we see that every child has these jealous cravings and of rivalry, together with his own feelings of guilt about them ; and that these are inherent in his weakness and dependence, and in the intensity and absoluteness of his feelings.

During all these years, between the end of the first and the sixth or seventh, this conflict is most acute. It is then that children have to take the biggest and most difficult step away from the primitive simplicity and intensity of their loves and hates, their hopes and fears, to some sort of controlled and social ways of behaviour ; and have to learn the hardest lesson of their lives, in accepting the fact that they cannot have exclusive possession of either or both of their parents, as the ways of infancy would demand.

The child will not be able to tell even the most sympathetic adult about his wishes and anxieties. They lie far too deep in him, beyond the reach of words. They come to him in wordless organic longings for caresses, in desires to remove and destroy, in fears of rejection and retaliation. The guilt and dread bound up with these complex shifting feelings are indeed so strong that the child has to keep his own thoughts turned away from them. He comes to deny in himself, not only *behaving* angrily or possessively, but even *wanting* to behave so.

Yet the longing to have his mother to himself in infantile ways, and his anger with his father or the rival child, spring from his deepest nature, and cannot be *annulled* by his guilt and fear. They can in time be tempered and socialised in their ways of expression; but, in the meantime, they and the guilt belonging to them find an outlet in roundabout ways, which we are only now beginning to understand.

**Fears and phantasies.** The child dreams of fierce animals eating him up, of giants and ogres, of huge engines running over him, and does not himself know that the fear of his father's punishments and his mother's anger is hidden behind these pictures. He may awaken from his dreams and nightmares shrieking with terror and bathed in sweat, and very commonly the content of these terrors is that " there are animals in the room, and in my bed—they'll bite my feet ". A boy of fourteen months woke thus in frantic fear that " a white rabbit was going to bite me ". (These fears of biting animals link up with the child's own angry biting impulses at the breast.) But often he cannot remember even so much of the imagined source of his terror, although his dread may be so great that he climbs out of his cot and cannot settle to sleep if left alone.

Such night-terrors are common in the second and third years, and may occur even earlier. And sometimes a little later, when the child is trying to overcome these terrors, he may lie sleepless until late at night, or awaken very early in the morning, and no change in the physical conditions of his life may for a time help him to sleep longer.

The child's deep and inarticulate conflicts may show themselves, too, in distaste for certain kinds of food, in bed-wetting, in inability to bear parting from his mother, or in storms of tears about small disappointments. Or they may be expressed in any one of the many *phobias* that spring up in little children, very often without any source in real events. The child develops a sudden and quite unreasoning fear of Christmas crackers or fireworks, of the noise the water makes going down from the bath, of the noise of the gas-meter, or noises in general. He may be frightened of the coalman, of horses and cows, of aeroplanes, of any quick-moving or flapping things, of the Punch and Judy show that all his friends are enjoying, of the rain or a waterfall. One child hates the smell of rubber so much that he gets frantic with anger and fear if made to wear mackintosh and Wellingtons. Another is terrified of a wireless set, and begs mother to " Shut the box so the man can't get out ". And a third goes into a paroxysm of crying if the grown-ups around him happen to laugh at anything he says—even if a moment before he was laughing himself.

The child's parents may in reality be kind and temperate and gentle, but his own imaginings are more real to him than any external fact. A poet has recently voiced this contrast between the real parents, and what they may be to the troubled phantasies of the little child :

THE INFANT

He tells his dreams, lifting his head in bed ;
" You were there with me, mother, and you said——"
" You and I raced together—you were last."
" I dreamt I hurt myself, but you went past."
" Some men attacked us, but you made them fly."
" No one was in the world but you and I."


All day I answer for my mood, my whim,
And put myself in shape to show to him.
But all the night God knows what I will do
At eve we play and kiss, but I know, too,
Tucking him in with smiles before we part,
That before morning I may break his heart.[1]

**Phantasy in play.**   There are very few children who
do not at some time or other show some or other of the
signs of these inward difficulties and perplexities.   If we
found a child who showed none, we should not be altogether happy about him, for we know that they must
be there, and that a child who was able to hide them
altogether was pledging his future mental health for
present success in living up to adult standards.

But many children of reasonable and understanding
parents are on the whole happy and friendly and loving,
with only occasional outbreaks of defiance or quarrelling
or unreasonable fears, or failures in cleanliness.   If we
watch such children at play, we shall see that their
play is the safety-valve for their hidden wishes and
fears.   Sometimes these are vividly expressed in family
games of papa and mamma and babies, with all the
rich drama of their phantasies underlined.   The make-

[1] By kind permission of Miss Viola Meynell and the Editor
of the *Observer*.

believe father and mother, for instance, are nearly always more severe and tyrannical than the real ones, and heartily scold and punish their " naughty " children. On the other hand, they are also infinitely tender and cherishing, and save their children from peril of lions and tigers, railway accidents, storms and drowning. They are equal to any dangers, all-wise and all-knowing. The little girl, with her family of babies whom she feeds and cares for and tyrannises over, the little boy, as the father of the family, the soldier, engine-driver, explorer, and big-game hunter, restore the balance of their own weakness and childishness ; and in punishing their play children or destroying the imagined wild animals they work out all sides of their own conflict.

The discharge in play of these inward tensions makes it easier for little children to temper their behaviour in real life. This is the one of the chief functions of play to which I have referred. And sad it is for those children whose anxiety is so great that they cannot play. We may look upon the inability to join with other children in imaginative and creative play as one of the surest signs of grave inner difficulties that will sooner or later seriously disturb the mental life—no matter how well-behaved and controlled the child otherwise now seems to be.

**The real parents.** If, then, it be true that in their deepest phantasies, children are liable to fear and hate us, whatever we are in fact, does that mean that our real behaviour makes no difference to them ? Far from it. It is, indeed, of the utmost importance to them that we should be in reality gentle and just, kind, temperate and reasonable. This is the greatest help that as parents we can give them, towards learning to distinguish between their imaginings, desires and fears, and real things. If we are in truth cruel and cold, capricious, unjust and tyrannical, our children are justified of their phantasies—and will become like us in their turn.

# CHAPTER VII

## SOME ANSWERS TO PROBLEMS

TURNING now to some of our typical problems what difference does this deeper knowledge of the little child's inner life make to our practical handling of him ? Let me begin with one general question which arises in every nursery and Nursery School—the problem of obedience. Our new understanding does make a difference to our view of what this issue is.

**Obedience.** There can hardly be any question as to whether or not the little child should be expected to obey—*in some things and for some purposes*. The call for obedience, as and when it is needed, is part of the biological responsibility of the parent. It does not need to be justified. It has its roots deep in the nature of the child himself. Obedience comes quite naturally to him if we ask for it in the right way and the right season. And he is in fact lost and bewildered if he has not the support of a firm framework of life ordered for him.

But obedience is not an end in itself. It is a *means* of education, not a final purpose. And the whole question turns upon *what* we ask the child to obey in, and *how* we put our demands to him.

Many people's difficulties come from not being clear about these things beforehand. If we are muddled in our own minds as to why we want obedience, and when and how we want it, we are very likely to ask for it when it isn't really valuable. We may dig ourselves in about the wrong things. We may demand obedience in such a way that we actually stir contrariness or obstinacy. Or else our own uncertainties get passed on to the children, so that they never know whether or not we mean what we say. And when once parents and children have got into a vicious circle of scolding and nagging, defiance and contrariness, this is far from easy to break.

Now when we say the child " should obey ", we clearly can't mean that he should never do anything without being told, never have any way of his own. Nor that we want him to be docile to our mere whim and fancy. That would be sacrificing the whole of his future to our present convenience, and what a useless sort of person it would make him. What we imply when we say he should obey us is that our particular demands are reasonable and just, and that obeying them will be good for him. But it is well to be sure about this.

**The need for freedom.** Moreover, it is no less true that children need freedom and choice than that they need to obey, if they are to grow up responsible and independent beings. They learn to exercise responsibility by having it, just as they learn to walk by trying to walk, to swim by swimming, to dance by dancing. They can't learn to be controlled and responsible by mere teaching in words, nor by the power of our wishes —but only by their own efforts, corrected by their own experience. Just as the best teaching in, for example, cricket or French can only come home to the child by his own effort and actual experience, so all our maxims about being sensible and independent in social behaviour can only become effective if we translate them into concrete opportunity. Even the little child needs some measure of real responsibility.

The issue turns, then, first of all, upon *what* we ask children to obey in. And there would seem three sorts of happenings to consider. (*a*) Things in which we do ask for definite obedience. (*b*) Those in which we leave the child completely free choice. And (*c*) Contingent things, which are not properly to be looked upon as questions of obedience. In these, whilst we may have our own hopes and preferences, we cannot do more than *suggest* them, directly or indirectly, since the end in view is defeated if we try to compel them.

**The what of obedience.** To the first group belong all those things that make the settled framework of the child's life—the time for meals, for bath and bed, the demand for clean hands before a meal, for putting away playthings that are in everybody's way, for not touching other people's belongings without permission, not running across the high road, not hitting or biting, and so on and so forth. All these things are firmly based in the real grounds of the children's own health or safety, or of other people's genuine rights. There are many of them, enough to give all the theoretical training in obedience that seems so important to many people ; but far fewer than most people imagine.

When our demands rest upon this objective basis, we are far more likely to be both firm and patient than if we try to enforce obedience merely " for obedience' sake ", irrespective of the particular thing at issue.

There are many possibilities in the second group, possibilities of really free choice. Even the little child can, for instance, have the responsibility for the arrangement of his own toys in his own cupboard or playbox, the choice of what games to play in his playtime, of which playmates he will invite to tea, of what he will grow in his own piece of garden, of where to go on his afternoon walk (at least sometimes), of the spending of his own pocket money, no matter how little it be. And when we do give him the choice in this way, it should be a real choice, not a pretence of one. We should not snatch it back in the very act of giving, because the child's choice turns out to be different from ours.

In the third group, the contingent situations which cannot fruitfully be made a question of obedience, there would seem to be two sub-groups. First, such pleasant things as friendly greetings, gentleness, politeness and consideration for others, freedom from shyness and willingness to play with other children. We all long for our children to be polite and gentle and co-operative and sociable. But none of us can *command* these things, and it is worse than useless to try to compel them. We can suggest, and sometimes persuade, but we cannot order. We can sometimes command mere lip service, but that is of no value unless to salve the pride of some offended grown-up. True friendliness and consideration grows from within, and largely from the child's happy experience of *our* consideration and understanding. To make these things a matter of formal obedience is to belie them.

And secondly, there are those sorts of behaviour which are neurotic in origin, the meaning of which my readers may now have begun to glimpse. Nail-biting, stammering, sleeplessness, the various phobias—not one of these should be treated as a question of obedience. Nail-biting and stammering are far best left alone. Indeed, it is very important that parents and amateurs should never try to deal with stammering. It is invariably made worse if they try to correct it. Until such time as psychological treatment can be sought (and it should be as early as possible), no notice should be taken of the difficulty.

**Phobias.** How best can we deal with the phobias? Two things are to be remembered. First, that these irrational fears are quite out of the child's control, and are intensely real to him even if they seem foolish to us. And secondly, that they very often pass away of themselves in a year or two, if not badly handled.

We should therefore avoid the occasions of fear, as far as this can be done unobtrusively, without letting the child feel too sheltered. When occasions do arise, and the child is afraid, we should give him quiet comfort without any fuss, never scolding nor trying to make him feel ashamed of himself. If we scold or jeer, we may be inflicting a far greater cruelty than we realise. If we fuss in sympathy, we may encourage the child to exploit his fears. Quiet support and understanding without too much direct attention are the most likely things to help him grow out of these troubles. If, however, the phobias are very severe or linger too long, then we need the help of a psycho-analyst experienced with children.

In general, then, as regards obedience, we should take care neither to ask the child for more than he can give, and give without undue strain, nor to put into the *form* of real demands things which we are not in the end justified in insisting upon. It is as important to keep firmly, however gently, to any definite requests that we do make, as it is to make sure that the requests themselves are wise and helpful.

So much for the *what* of obedience.   And the *how* has to be considered too.

**The how of obedience.**   Do we remember, for instance, when making our requests, how much less sense of past and future the young child has, and how much more he lives in the immediate present than we do ?   If we remember this, we shall also remember how much more urgent his desires are than ours, and how much sharper a disappointment or a denial is to him than to us.   And since he is necessarily given up more completely to anything in which he is interested, without thought of time and place, it means much more to him than to us when we have to interrupt what he is doing because we want him, for example, to come to dinner or to go out for a walk.   If we remember this, we shall not wantonly and suddenly cut across his interests, but shall give him a little notice, so that he has time to take in the request.   If, as an example, when he is in the middle of an absorbing game, and we have to call him to come to a meal, we can give him a few minutes' warning, " In ten minutes it will be dinner-time ", he is much more likely to come cheerfully and readily than if we can tell him only at the very moment we want him to come, and expect him to do it on the instant.   We ourselves hate to be suddenly interrupted when we are reading or talking to a friend.   The child hates it too.   And he appreciates our consideration very keenly.   Such consideration can quite well go along with firmness about the request when the time comes for acting upon it— and this too the child appreciates.   Courtesy on our part does not mean weakness ; nor is a thoughtless lack of consideration for the child's real limitations by any means the same thing as firmness.

Again, having made sure that we are asking the right thing, do we take it for granted in a cheerful voice and friendly manner that he will do what we wish ? Or do we show him by a doubtful or fretful tone that we are rather *expecting* him to grumble or defy us ? If we ourselves are calm and friendly in our demands, he is more likely to agree, and to do what we want in the same friendly and cheerful way. But we *can* only be calm and confident when we are really sure that what we are asking is reasonable and just.

And it is well, with the very young child, not to be too ready to treat any momentary defiance as an immediate occasion for a pitched battle of wills, but to give him a little time to get over his contrariness, wherever this is practicable. If when he says " shan't " to a request, we say " Perhaps you will do it later on ? " in most cases he will.

If the child shows open defiance, rage and tantrums, there is still no need for *us* to scold or rage. It is useless to shake him and say, " Stop screaming ", and much the best to wait patiently until the crying and screaming is done and then make our request again—provided only it was a necessary and reasonable one. The important thing is to make sure that the child gains nothing from his tantrums. Such storms of open defiance are very common towards the end of the second year of growth and for a year or two later, even in children who have been placid babies. They seem to be largely an early form of self-assertion, that passes away as the child comes to greater skill and social ease. They are trying enough at the time, but an atmosphere of calm and firm patience and steady affection helps them to disperse.

**Feeding difficulties.** Let me take now the diffi-

culties so often cropping up in the second and third
years as regards food and feeding.  For example, the child
who refuses to eat after the birth of a new baby, or who
suddenly and without any apparent reason becomes
contrary about his food.  The best way is undoubtedly
to leave the child to eat by himself and not to try to
force or coax.  Whenever we do try to coax or force the
child because we think we know the amount he should
eat, what we are really doing is to come between the
child and his food, and to keep the thing a complicated
*social* question, rather than letting it be a more direct
relation between the child and his food.  If the child is
not ill or sickening for any illness, and if the food is of
the right kind and attractively cooked, and the child
is left to eat it or not as he wishes, he almost always will
(apart from very rare cases of severe psychological disturbance) eat what his appetite demands.  He will nearly
always eat more when left to himself and the food than
when nurse or mother tries to insist on his eating, and
he will digest and assimilate what he has eaten far
better.

It is, of course, always important to have medical
advice as to his general health, making sure that his
refusal to eat is not a preliminary symptom of bodily
illness.

Whenever I am asked about this, I wish I could do
with mother or nurse what is quite often done in some
of the splendid Nursery Schools in America, where they
have made a careful scientific study of all such problems.
Certain of these schools are staffed by experienced
teachers and psychologists and doctors, who have gained
the closest co-operation of the mothers of the children.
They have a special screen across one end of the room

(as described in Chapter IV), which is transparent in one direction and opaque in the other, so that the mothers and visitors can watch without the children being disturbed by their presence. By means of this mothers have the rare chance of seeing their children as they are by themselves, or rather, as they behave in the hands of highly trained and experienced educators. And this question of feeding is the one that has been most often helped and improved by this method.

When a mother comes to the school saying, " My Tommy won't eat. You'll never get him to touch his dinner. He doesn't like this, and he won't eat that. He never eats anything unless I stand over him and make him "—such a mother is given the opportunity of seeing just how her boy does behave when amongst the other children he is given a dish of the right sort of food, and left alone to eat it or not. The head of one of these schools was recently describing to me how a particular mother had behaved under these circumstances. She sat behind the screen watching the children, and when she saw her Tommy opposite a plate of food like the other children, she said, " He will never eat that, he never touches carrots at home ". But presently she saw him take up his spoon and begin to eat like the other children around him. When she saw a glass of milk of the prescribed size put beside the boy she said, " Well, anyhow he won't drink that ", and was surprised when Tommy actually did drink the milk. There were no adults at Tommy's table ; he was just alone with three or four children, and as there was nobody to mind whether he ate or not, or to scold and fuss if he did not, his appetite acted naturally, and he ate his food with enjoyment. And the mother went home really believing for the first time that it was far better not to make a fuss, and not to treat the question as one of obedience and disobedience.

**Lying.** Another practical problem, one about which most parents let themselves be unwisely distressed, is that of lying.

All children tell untruths at some time or other ; but their lies are of several sorts, and before we can deal with any one we need to know what it sprang from. The very young child will " lie " through the vividness of his imagination, either because he cannot yet distinguish between phantasy and reality, or because he loves the game of pretending. There is no need to do anything about this—time and growth will do it for us. It is useful sometimes to reply to his exaggerations with an obviously amused " Is it ? " " Did you ? "—entering into the game with him, and letting him feel from our tone that we appreciate that it is a game.

The somewhat older child may lie either in self-defence or from a desire for self-enlargement. If the lie springs from fear, this usually means either that our way of dealing with the behaviour which he denies (perhaps breaking or losing something) is too severe, or that for some reason or other he has lost general confidence in us. To scold or punish for the lying itself is in this case to foment the very trouble from which it sprang ; and may only mean that the intelligent child will be careful to lie more skilfully. Nothing can help until we have convinced the child that his fears have no basis, and given him back his belief in our love and reasonableness. It is therefore better to ignore the lying itself, beyond making a simple comment that if he sometimes lies we shan't know when he is telling the truth ;

and to turn our attention to the grounds of his fear, and ways of removing them.

The boastful lie can best be dealt with in much the same way. One may, perhaps, make a rather stronger protest here, and bring home to the child how awkward it may be for him if we cannot tell when he is speaking the truth and when not ; but the main attack must again be indirect. If a child feels the need to boast, or to make an impression by lying, then he is suffering under some sense of weakness and inferiority. It is for us to find out, if possible, what lies behind this, and to remedy it by giving him confidence in himself. Perhaps he has not enough opportunities for real achievement ; or perhaps we are saying " Don't " too often. As in the case of so many special difficulties of child training, the remedy lies more in a revision of our general ways of dealing with the child than in a specific attack on the particular difficulty. Habitual or frequent lying in any child is a sure indication that his surroundings, and his relations with his parents, need overhauling. If the child goes on with it after we have made sure that we are ourselves behaving gently, reasonably and consistently, it means that he is deeply disturbed in his emotional life, and that we need to seek the advice of a specialist in psychological difficulties.

**Masturbation.** We may now look again at the difficult question we raised in our chapter of problems —what to do when we find the child of three or four playing with his genital organ. And the answer is—do nothing directly. For we can now see that this is but another expression of the intense inner conflict of the child's feelings towards his parents. In the course of the struggle to overcome his desire for absolute possession of his mother, and his sense of rivalry with his otherwise loved father, the child sometimes takes refuge in self-stimulation, with secret and inarticulate phantasies of satisfaction. He has neither words nor the knowledge of himself to tell us this ; nor have we come to understand it without long and patient study of the whole facts of human sexual development. We now know however that this action, so distressing to most parents, is nevertheless a common thing in the ordinary course of development. But just because it is bound up with the most hidden issues of the child's emotional life, we must go very slowly in dealing with it ; and are far more likely to do harm by rushing in to scold or correct than by leaving the child to deal with it himself—in a general atmosphere of calm goodwill and friendly interest in all his outward concerns. For the child *always* feels ashamed and distressed about it. Our main task is very definitely to avoid strengthening the fear and guilt that go along with it, for these rivet the child but the more firmly in the habit. As a leading medical authority has said, about the same thing in the years of later youth, " It is, further, beyond all doubt that by far the greater part of the harmful features often associated with undue auto-erotism are the result, not of the phenomena themselves, but of the conflicts arising from the mental attitude towards them." [1] The children who become real " cases " demanding special treatment are more usually those who have early been scolded or whipped or severely punished for their first attempts. Or, most seriously of all, those who have been threatened by parent or nurse that their organ " will be cut off " for the act. Nothing

[1] Dr. Ernest Jones, in the Foreword to *Auto-Erotic Phenomena in Adolescence*, by K. Menzies.

could be more harmful or terrible to the child than this malicious threat. And rarely, if ever, do any of these methods achieve the desired end. Our ways must thus be indirect. We can give the child nothing better than friendly companionship and calm affection, expressed, however, in a sympathetic sharing of his games and stories and questioning interest in the outer world, rather than in bodily caresses. Indeed, these latter should at all times be sparing. If we indulge *our* love for the child by excessive kissing and caressing, rather than by intelligent provision for his interest in things and events, we cannot be surprised when he fails to leave behind his own primitive modes of affection.

If the habit persists, and is more than an occasional thing—for this will happen sometimes even with children of excellent parents in the happiest home—then all that remains to us as parents is to ask the advice of a specialist in psychological treatment. We cannot do more ourselves, for, being his parents, we are the storm-centre of his emotional problem, and cannot pilot him through it. Only by uncovering the deeper sources of the trouble can the child then be helped to master it ; and this is the most delicate and difficult task in human relations, to be undertaken only by the most highly skilled and experienced persons.

Very closely connected with this problem is another general consideration which has to be kept in mind throughout these early years—the avoidance of wanton stimulation of the child's conflict on our part. Sometimes we do this thoughtlessly—by, for instance, letting our secret preference for another of our children show itself in voice or caress or uneven justice ; sometimes even more thoughtlessly, by teasing the jealous child about his pain. Parents who are wise and kind enough to avoid these pitfalls, however, and who are sensibly sparing of caresses, will sometimes slip into another serious error— and that is, letting a child of more than a few months sleep in the same room as themselves. Sometimes this is even done with children of four, or more, years of age —under the illusion that they are too young to have any interest in the relations of the parents. Those who have studied very closely all the inner life of little children are now quite clear that this *is* an error and an illusion, and one which increases the child's difficulties. He does not, of course, fully understand what their relation is ; but he senses its intimate character, interprets this according to his own deep organic longings and infantile memories, and feels shut out of what he wants and what they enjoy. Children under these circumstances—even children of less than two years of age—are far more observant and watchful than their parents imagine. They lie awake listening when seemingly asleep, or start up in anxious desire to see what is hidden from them ; and ponder and imagine and dream and desire, in secret bewilderment. They have, of course, some time or other to accept the fact that their parents have a special relation into which they may not enter, and from which spring their brothers and sisters ; but to be brought so closely up against the fact makes it harder for them. Most of us would see this as obvious, if we did not rest content in the widespread error that our children did not " think about such things ".

It can be said dogmatically that on this and other grounds of bodily and mental health, every child should, if possible, have a bedroom to himself from the beginning ; but particularly, that he should not share his parents' room.

**Where do babies come from ?** One of our most important problems was how to deal with the child's questions as to where babies come from. We can perhaps now see that it is quite indispensable to the child to have his questions frankly and simply answered, at the time when he asks them.

What happens in the child's mind if he asks his questions trustingly and gets no answer, an evasive answer, or an answer that he will sooner or later (and it is usually sooner rather than later) find out to be untrue ?

If he gets no answer, or an evasive one, he is lost and bewildered by the sense that his grown-up friends either don't know the most important things that he wants to understand, or (and this is the more probable) that they won't tell him. And if they won't tell him, *why* won't they ? It can only be that there is something wrong and shameful about the knowledge they withhold. And indeed, the voice and tone and expression of mother when she told him to " hush " and " not to ask such things ", or turned away and talked of something else, did suggest that there was something dark and strange about it. Then that means that behind this story of being small and growing, behind the question of where one comes from, behind the love of mother and father and even mother's love for the child himself, is something shameful and hidden, too shameful and hidden to be spoken of. What can it be ? And in this way, the springs of life and love may be poisoned for the child. What could be more destructive of goodness and happiness than to be led to believe that one's own very existence was rooted in shameful mystery ?

If we tell actual untruths, he is bound to find it out sooner or later, and we cannot then expect him to tell the truth to us.  How bad for the child to discover, not merely that mother would not help him to understand, but that she would rather let herself tell a lie to him than answer his groping questions !  Very many of the lies of children spring from their justified loss of confidence in their parents about this, and their quick perception that we preach one thing and practise another.

It is the foundation of the child's confidence in us as true helpers and honest friends that is at stake.  It is worth a little trouble on our part to find the best way of answering.

When the child says, therefore, " Where did I come from ? " surely the only possible reply is the true one, put into simple words that he can understand.  " You grew in a warm nest inside me until you were big enough to grow without me, and so you were born."  And when he asks who looked after him when his mother was " little ", the answer is that he was not here then ;  he was not then made, and had not begun to grow inside his mother.  And all this can be linked up with the life of the animals he loves to play with, or to watch in the fields—the lamb and the foal, the kitten and puppy. They also grow inside " a warm nest " in their mothers, growing safely and happily there until they are big enough and strong enough to eat and move about by themselves.

But the best way to help the child understand all this is, of course, to let him keep pet animals and their young. Mice and rabbits are delightful pets for this purpose, and quite easy to manage if one has a garden or outdoor shed.  A hen and a sitting of eggs in the spring also help to make things clear ;  and besides giving the child great pleasure, they make the opportunity to explain that birds of all sorts lay eggs, and then keep the eggs warm in an outside nest they have built for them ; whereas cats and dogs and mice and many other animals do like ourselves, and keep the young ones even safer than the baby bird in the egg, warm and cosy inside the mother herself.

A great many mothers nowadays are dealing with the problem on these lines, and finding them most satisfactory. Many are keeping notes of all the questions their little children ask about babies, and of how they take the knowledge that is given them in reply. When a new baby is coming, the child is presently told about it, and of how it is growing safely inside the mother. The child's interest and pleasure in the prospect of a new playmate is encouraged, and any questions about how it grows, and what it will be like when it is born, and so on, are answered simply and frankly. And in every case, there is no shadow of doubt that this frank simplicity and comradeship of the mother has excellent results on the child's mind.

Most people feel the father's part in procreation to be the most delicate and difficult aspect of the problems. There is no particular age at which children become interested in this. Some ask about it earlier, and some later ; some never ask at all, but come to their own conclusions about things. The only guide for the parent is the child's own interest and questions. *If* he asks, then he must be answered about this, just as much as about the mother's part, and just as simply and truthfully. The father plants the seed which the mother shelters and nourishes, and which presently grows into the little baby. The child is intuitively prepared to receive this knowledge by his spontaneous interest in the family relationships of animals, as well as by his immediate sense of the special closeness of " daddy and mummy and baby ".

" Daddy and mummy " co-operate in beginning the life
of the infant, no less than they do in loving him and
caring for his needs after he is born.   Why should the
essential meaning of the special relationship of fatherhood
be clothed in shadow and mystery, any more than that
of motherhood ?   Sooner or later children have to come
to know this too.   Let it be learnt from wise and understanding parents, rather than from hole-and-corner
informants !

Briefly, then, we may say that there are at least the
following two fundamental reasons for dealing with the
child's questions as clearly and straightforwardly as we
possibly can : (a) Only by so doing can we keep the
child's confidence and belief in our love and genuine
desire to help him.   It is no good our *telling* the child
we love him, and then failing to meet his needs.   He
knows whether we love him or not, by our behaviour
to him.   He will sense our true wish to meet his difficulties and help him understand, or our fear and evasion
and unwillingness.

(b) The great value of knowledge of the biological
unity of human life with life as a whole, and the facts
of biology in general.   What serious grounds can there
be for failing to open up to the child's interest and
understanding such an essential field of knowledge ?   He
naturally has an intuitive sense of his oneness with the
animals he loves.   Who could doubt the child's spontaneous delight in other living creatures who had ever
seen children with their own pets, watched their eager
interest at the Zoo, or told them stories of animals ?
And it is the family relationship of animals that chiefly
wins their attention in the early years, " the little baby
pigs " ; " the daddy and mummy bear ", the cow and her

calf, the mother swallow feeding her young. These things make it relatively easy to help the child understand the story of human birth and are much better than long explanations by the parents. I would have families of animals in every kindergarten and school and home if it were in my power to arrange it ! Even in his early years, the child can be gathering knowledge about animal life which is a joy in itself, and an intellectual stimulus to further effort and inquiry, and which will later lead on to the more serious study of all those facts of biology which underlie health and disease, both in man (e.g., in modern infant welfare itself), and in the plants and animals upon which his life depends.

In this, I am, of course, looking many years ahead for the little child. The four- and five-year-old is interested only to feed and watch and play with animals, and to sow his seeds and gather the blossom and fruit of the garden. But these are the beginnings of what may in later years become a serious pursuit and permanent intellectual delight, to add to the pleasures of literature and art and music. What a pity not to open the door to such a range of knowledge and pleasure ! But we may shut that door, if we do not let the little child enjoy contact with living creatures, if we bar his interest to some of the central facts of their lives, the facts of mating and parenthood, or if we deny him knowledge of human birth and make him turn away in shame from his own origin, instead of letting him feel the vast interest and beauty of the great pageant of life as a whole.

**The age for answering.** A point often raised is the age at which to give the child the true answer. Some people suggest that six or seven is better than three or four. But surely the only age is the one when the child asks ! There is no particular virtue in six as against three. If the child does not ask until six or seven, well and good ; but if he does (and the age in fact varies a good deal according to the child and the circumstances), then it can only do harm to postpone the answer, on grounds the child cannot possibly understand. To do so is to give a false weight to the curiosity, and will usually only make him hide it. If the child does ask at three, it means that he is unusually intelligent and observant, or that some special circumstance has drawn his attention to the problem. And (as far as I have been able to observe) he will nearly always have thought a good deal about the question *before* he asks. That means he is ready for the answer, no matter how young he be. I have no doubt that all of us greatly under-estimate the intelligence and power of observation of young children—largely, perhaps, because it suits us to do so !

**Fairy-tales.** One last point : People sometimes seem to fear that if children know these truths about the origin of babies, they will not want to play imaginative games, nor be interested in fairy-tales. Some have even implied that those educators who think that the truth about these things is essential do not believe in fairy-tales in general. But neither of these suggestions is sound. Little children go on playing their imaginative games of " mummy and daddy and the children " just as freely and happily when they know that babies spring from the mutual love of daddy and mummy, and are sheltered and nourished in mother's body before birth, as if they had been told about storks or gooseberry bushes. Indeed, they often seem to play *more* freely and imaginatively—*because they are less afraid of their* *own thoughts*, and of what mummy would say if she knew them ! The children of truthful parents will of course not play at " storks ", but they will invent endless games of mother and father and the babies, of nurse and doctor, of washing and feeding the baby, putting him to sleep, taking him for walks, visiting and going picnics, etc., etc. This greater freedom of the imagination in dramatic play is one of the very boons which mother's sympathetic understanding of the child's interest in babies, and her kind honesty in answering questions, is able to bring to the child. It is when mother suggests that the subject is taboo that the child's imaginative play is more likely to become inhibited.

Nor is the value of fairy-tales in general in the least affected by this question of the truth about real events. No one who knows little children could wish to deprive them of the joys of the fairy-tale, as imaginative experience and as literature, any more than one would wish to deprive the grown-up of imaginative art in painting and poetry and drama and the novel, because of the growth of scientific knowledge ! We do not need to believe that stories and plays are real historical truth in order to enjoy them ! Nor do they give us less delight because we also take pleasure in the facts of biology or astronomy or actual human history. And the little child goes on loving his fairy-stories, and having as much imaginative need of them, when he understands the true facts about important real things. Indeed, he can let his imagination roam all the more freely because his real life is firmly rooted in truth and honesty. He is not for ever wondering whether what his parents say is *true*, and does not feel so perplexed about where the real ends and " pretending " begins. He can give himself up to " let's

pretend ", and to the convention of the story, with the
same security that we have when we yield to the magic
of the theatre or the novel.   To share imaginative literature with the child, and to tell him untruths about real
events, are two quite different things, which it is very
important to distinguish.

**The emotional problem.**   After all this, however,
we must not imagine that even such wise and friendly
methods will make everything perfectly smooth and easy
for *all* our children.   Knowledge can do much, and the
frank simplicity of the parents which makes knowledge
possible can do more ; but the child's central emotional
problem remains his own.   Whatever he knows or does
not know, he still has to learn his hardest lesson—to give
up the possessive and primitive ways of infancy for
tempered social relations.   And some children, even of
wise and moderate and kindly parents, find this beyond
their strength.   In spite of all our care, their conflicts
are more than they can manage, and they take refuge in
persistent tantrums or fears or lying or loss of control.
When this happens, we have to turn for help to others,
to those who have made remedial work with young
children their profession.   Indeed, it is not a small part
of intelligent parenthood to know when such help is
called for.

**Companionship in play.**   Finally, one great help we
can give our children is the companionship of other
children in play.   No matter how friendly and successful
our own relation with them is, they need other children,
as we have seen in discussing the only child.   We ourselves press too heavily upon them by the mere fact of
being adults.   With other children, they can work out
their phantasies more freely, in their dramatic games,

and in making and doing together ; and can get real, concrete experience of social relations, on their own level of desire and control. They learn, for example, that other people's wishes are also real, and that if there are leaders there must be followers—in a way that no words of ours can teach. For some part of every day, young children between infancy and ordinary school age should enjoy a time of free play with other children, not very much older or younger. This is one of the many ways in which the Nursery School is valuable—and not only for children whose alternative is playing in the streets. It is no less a boon for children of comfortable homes and gardens, in these days of small families. The need for companionship is as great as the need for shelter and comfort ; and, if no Nursery School is at hand, we must find ways of joining in with other parents to ensure that their children and ours are able to come together for free play as often as possible.

And in that time of play, they should be as free from grown-up interference as possible. We may stand by, to learn our own lesson of what children say and do when left to themselves, but we must not be obviously watching them ; and must refrain from telling them what to do and what not to do, within the real limits of physical safety. So we shall have some chance of gaining a fuller knowledge of children in general, and of our own children in particular. And without that knowledge how shall we guide them ?

# CHAPTER VIII

## PLAYTHINGS

HAVING now made clear the general point of view which should decide, among other things, our choice of play material for little children, I can be entirely practical in this chapter. Much of what I say will of course be a commonplace to many people ; but some of my suggestions may happen to be new to some readers —and it is always useful to remind ourselves of the particular values even of familiar things.

The first and most obvious (yet often forgotten) point is that the things we give to children should be chosen because they meet the children's need, not because they may amuse our idle moments. They must be suited to the children's interest and pleasure at their particular stage of development—which means that we must put some thought into the buying, not leaving their choice to a salesman of the latest fashion in toys.

I have already described suitable playthings for the one-year child, and will here deal with the needs of two- to six-year children.

From the third to the seventh year, the playthings children need can be usefully put into four broad groups, although these naturally overlap.

1. **Things which help physical growth.** Many of the ordinary things in house and garden will be used

for climbing and jumping if we do not prevent it—and if we want to prevent it, we must provide others for the purpose. An old box firmly placed, with a movable board for running up and jumping off or sliding down (all wooden things given to children should be planed and free from splinters or nails) ; a short step-ladder— a fixed one is best at first, then later a light ladder which the children can carry about ; a low railing for climbing on and balancing ; a wooden cart to trundle about ; a set of ninepins ; a swing, and later a see-saw of proper height (if this has hooks fixed underneath on which weights can be hung, the older children will learn to weigh each other on it) ; a firmly built wooden frame with horizontal rods to climb on and hang from ; an old tree-trunk or group of logs—and presently actual trees to climb ; balls to throw and kick, hoops to run with ; and, at five or six years, a bat and skipping-rope.

The climbing frame, light ladders and sliding boards are best made by a local carpenter or ladder-maker. They would be cheaper from such a source than from any educational supply firm. The essential points about a good climbing frame are that it must be firmly based and perfectly stable, that the cross-bars on which the children climb must be perfectly smooth and free from splinters, and of the right diameter for small hands to grasp firmly ; and that the spaces between the uprights should be large enough for the children to get in and out, and climb through easily. With such a frame or cage, a group of small children will play most happily for long periods—climbing up and down, stretching their arms and taking the weight of their bodies off their legs (always a good thing), hanging upside down and in all positions, and in general getting splendid exercise as well as lots of fun ; and sometimes turning the whole thing into a house or cubby-hole, with rugs and cushions, for make-believe play.

Several of these things, such as the see-saw, the ladders, and the climbing frame, are more easily arranged for by the Nursery School, or by a group of parents, than by any one parent of ordinary means. But this is scarcely a disadvantage, if it leads a group of families to join together in providing better play room and playthings than any one can provide alone—especially as the needed companionship of other children will thus also be assured.

2. **Material for making things.** (a) Prepared things such as bricks and beads are more easily used than raw material (except plasticine) in the years 2–4. Wooden bricks of various sizes and shapes for piling up, building and various floor games ; wooden blocks of different shapes (cubes, prisms, discs, rods, etc.), with holes pierced, into which wooden pegs can be put for holding them together (both bricks and blocks should be ordered as wanted from the local carpenter, who will be able to make them more cheaply than they are bought in the shops, and to required sizes) ; hollow building blocks made of old cigar boxes glued or wired together—with a supply of these large and light blocks, children can make " real " playhouses to sit in ; large coloured wooden beads, an inch or more in diameter, or a number of empty cotton reels painted different colours, to be threaded on string or wire, in the third year ; and later, smaller (but not small) wooden and glass beads, to be threaded with a bodkin or darning needle, and thick coloured thread ; coloured sticks which can be stuck together with plasticine. (Children soon discover the adhesive value of plasticine.) " Tinker-Toy " and

" Pick-a-bricks " are a good sort of toy, too, for later on.

" Meccano," excellent for older children, is not suitable for children under six, for it needs finer handling than they can wisely be encouraged to give. On the same grounds, the old-fashioned kindergarten sewing cards with fine holes, sometimes still given to children, are to be wholly condemned.

(b) Of raw material, the one children can earliest use and longest delight in, is clay ; and the best form of clay for these early years is plasticine, since it keeps soft and usable all the time. Even two-year-olds will delight in rolling it in their fingers, and giving names to the forms accidentally produced. Then they will begin to make " worms " and " snakes " and other animals, and men ; and presently go on to cups and plates for use in " make-believe " ; and to houses and farms and boats and engines. At five or six, they will be ready to make more permanent things with clay that sets hard—bowls and jars and dishes ; and to paint these in design ; and to model gardens and landscapes, using shells and sticks and marbles with the clay. A small rolling-pin is a good tool to use with plasticine, and old tin lids are useful for cutting out flat discs. Through all these years, children enjoy play with sand and water, and a sand-pile in a sunny corner can be looked upon as a necessity of childhood. If this can be in a sunken pit of brick, which has a tap of running water (the handle should be removable, for days when water is *not* desirable), and the children have buckets and trowels or wooden (not iron) spades (no sharp corners), and clothes that will not spoil, or none at all, they can be in paradise for many hours on any sunny day. Old bottles and corks, and a length of rubber tubing, give rise to many interesting experiments. If the pit is not possible, the sand-pile should be boarded round on three sides to prevent the sand scattering.

Gardening tools for the years 4–6 should be light but strong; a barrow to carry sand or soil or dead leaves, a rake, broom, small trowel and fork. A small size of proper tools is a far better investment than those sold as toys for children, which are always of poor stuff and quickly broken. A trowel, being easily handled and having round edges, is better than a spade.

Paper is always welcome—coloured tissue for making streamers and dressing dolls, at first; stiffer paper for cutting out and making into dolls and houses, with pins or paste, later on; thin cardboard can be used for some purposes at five or six; newspaper all the time, in endless ways. Large sheets of brown or of rough kitchen paper can be made into books by folding and fastening them together with coarse " Sylko " thread sewn through and tied. The children can then paste in cut-out pictures, or their own paintings.

The children might keep a stock of old newspapers in their own cupboard.

Children of three will try to use scissors (which should have rounded ends), and will enjoy simply cutting up (as well as tearing), e.g. newspaper. The so-called " Kindergarten " scissors sold at twopence a pair are however quite useless, as they never will cut. A more usable pair can be bought for sixpence. Later on, discarded catalogues of motor-car, fancy goods and other manufacturers are much prized for cutting out.

The first sewing stuff should be large-holed canvas, with bodkins and coloured thread. Then soft, cheap, coloured cotton stuff, large pieces of it (or pieces of old dresses), to be made into bags or mats or dusters or curtains or aprons, and decorated with large beads or stitches. If children are allowed to use and wear the things they make, they will quite early (four or five years) succeed in making aprons, jumpers, dusters, bags, curtains, scarves, handkerchiefs and nightdress cases, which will hold together and give *them* pleasure, even if the stitches are an inch or two long, and there are many gaps in the seams. Coloured raffia can be used to sew with the canvas, and wrapped over cardboard to make rings and mats and boxes, or twisted into string. Children of five and six also enjoy weaving, " making stuff " with coloured wool on small cardboard looms.

At five and six years, or even earlier with careful supervision, children are ready to use hammer and nails and saw. Here, again, " toy " tools sold for children are worthless, a small size of real tools being far safer and more lasting. The tools should be well balanced, and of the right size and weight. The young child will enjoy simply knocking nails in (these should be flat-headed) ; but if he has a variety of pieces of wood—small and large blocks of varying thickness, one or two small planks, a few plasterer's laths, empty cotton reels for use as wheels—he will soon begin to make things, an aeroplane or motor-car, for example. These will be of the crudest design and execution, but that is his own affair.

The need for large material must be particularly re-membered when choosing drawing and painting things. Not only is this wiser on physiological grounds, it is far more fruitful æsthetically, at this age. A blackboard, say, 3 feet by 4 feet, fixed on the wall at the right height, will cost a few shillings, but is very durable, and remains useful all through childhood. The surface can easily be renewed with a mixture of glue, flour, emery and lamp-black. Or in default of the board, a piece of plain brown linoleum does very well. Thick coloured chalks can be used with this, as well as with large sheets of brown paper (from household parcels, for instance). For white drawing-paper, cheap kitchen paper bought by the roll does very well, and is better than good quality paper if this has to be given in small sheets for economy. Crayons should be in wood—the soft breakable ones are useless for small children ; and thick carpenter's pencils are the best in the beginning. Paint should be in liquid form, ready mixed, in small jars, for the solid blocks in small boxes are too difficult to manage. " Show-card colours " are the most useful. A thing most children love is to paint their own tables and chairs and boxes with " real " (house-painter's) paint. Even small children will get pleasing colour designs with this material. It has, of course, to be done out of doors, in old clothes of no value ; and a stock of turpentine kept ready for clean-ing hands afterwards.

Many of these different materials can be brought together into continuous pursuits—such as making and furnishing a dolls' house. Given a large soap- or orange-box (which first has all the splinters planed off), the children could with a little help turn it into a delightful dolls' house. An old book of wall-paper can always be got from a decorator's, and small pieces could be pasted on to the wall of the different rooms. Floor mats could be made by fringing bits of old serge or canvas. Match-boxes glued together in different ways will make tables and chairs and cupboards ; charming furniture can be made from chestnuts, with pins stuck in them for legs and backs, and coloured wool woven through the pins in a pattern. Coloured curtains and bed-coverings of cretonne or muslin can be sewn with large stitches ; jars and lamps and dishes can be modelled with plasticine or glitter-wax. Pictures can be crayoned or painted for the walls. An endless variety of delightful occupations can be found in furnishing and decorating the dolls' home. If added to as new things are learnt, it will yield fun and activity for years. But the doing of all this should, needless to say, never be forced, or made into " lessons ".

Another thing which even four- and five-year-olds can manage, if grown-ups are patient, is cooking— " real " cooking. They might sometimes, e.g., stew fruit, or make buns for their own tea with materials they themselves buy at a shop.

3. **Phantasy material**, used in " make-believe ", includes the ordinary toys most children have—the dolls' houses (whether home-made or bought) and dolls, engines, motor-cars, aeroplanes, trains, signals, and the like. It is not necessary to buy costly or elaborate things for young children. The boy of six does, of course, appreciate his " Hornby " engine, but for his younger brother, a larger wooden one is better. The two- and three-year-old will love a Noah's Ark with a set of animals. Cheap wooden toys are in general better than cheap tin ones, as they last longer and have not sharp edges.

In this group of playthings, we may include also chairs and tables which are made into trains, houses, shops, tunnels and steamers, etc. If children are not to use the ordinary furniture in their play, old or cheap second-hand chairs, e.g., can be given to them. Here we may also put all the old junk, worthless to the grown-ups, which children love to keep, odds and ends of silk lace and ribbon, old " dressing-up " clothes, old wooden or cardboard boxes, discarded pans and cans, detached wheels, parts of clocks or disused household things, boxes of old buttons and trimmings, old books (these are very useful for building tunnels and bridges)—all or any of these are used from time to time in " make-believe ", and can be stored in an old trunk or box.   Old cushions, rugs and pillows are prized for making beds when " playing house ".

4. **Formal material,** for getting to know geometrical shapes and sizes, and counting.  This includes such things as sets of blocks graded in size, like Dr. Montessori's tower of ten cubes, and her sets of cylinders graded in height and diameter ;  various kinds of " form-board ", having different shaped holes and blocks to fit them, for sorting ;  a series of wire rods fixed in a frame, and graded in size so as to hold from 1–10 large wooden beads, which the children can take on and off in counting ;  or a series of graded wooden rods, running from 1–10 centimetres (or inches) in length ;  bags of shells or bone counters, and bundles of coloured sticks —with printed number cards to go with them ;  a tape-measure and folding footrule ;  a pair of household scales, and silver sand for weighing.  This type of plaything has very great charm and value for little children, and can easily be graded to the stage of development reached, which in its turn it serves to measure clearly and accurately. The reader should turn to *Dr. Montessori's Own Hand-book* for a full description of her special set of apparatus. The same type of toy can easily be made by the home carpenter.   A wide variety of formal play material can

now also be obtained from the Auto-Education Institute (113, Islington Row, Birmingham, 15).[1]

It is not, of course, suggested that children should have all or most of the playthings described all at once. From those mentioned a choice can be made according to means and circumstance.  And it is to be remembered that the more costly toys do not necessarily give the greatest satisfaction to children.  The " old junk " plaything is in fact turned to more constantly than any other.

Finally, it is a wise general rule to leave the children free to use their playthings in their own way—even if this does not happen to be the way that we might think the best.  For play has the greatest value for the young child when it is really free and his own.

[1] See p. 138 for American sources of supply.

Don't merely say, " You mustn't do *that* " if you can possibly add " but you may do *this* ".

Don't call a thing " naughty " when you mean merely " it's a nuisance to me ".

Don't discuss children in front of them ; nor in general assume that they won't listen or notice or understand.

Don't interrupt anything the child is doing without giving him fair warning.

Don't show your love by constantly caressing the child, but by providing for his interests.

Don't " take " the child for a walk—go with him.

Don't hesitate to make holidays to rules sometimes.

Don't make a display of your concern when the child falls down, won't eat, etc.  Do what is needed instead of fussing and worrying.

Don't tease or use sarcasm—laugh *with* the child, but not *at* him.

Don't show off with the child to others, nor make him a plaything.

Don't give moral lectures to the small child ; if you find yourself doing this, don't be surprised or angry if he shows that he is bored.

Don't assume that the child understands what you are saying to him just because you do.

Don't, if you say or do something in anger, pretend that you did it " for the child's good " ; humbug does more harm than honest ill-temper.

Don't break promises, or make any you may not be able to keep.

Don't lie or evade.

# BOOKS FOR REFERENCE

## THE GENERAL FACTS OF DEVELOPMENT

Ballard, P. B. *Mental Tests*. London: Hodder & Stoughton.

Baldwin and Stecher. *The Psychology of the Pre-School Child*. New York: Appleton-Century-Crofts.

Freud, Sigmund. *Introductory Lectures on Psycho-analysis*. London: Allen & Unwin.

Gesell, Arnold. *The Mental Growth of the Pre-School Child*. London: Macmillan.

———. *Infancy and Human Growth*. London: Macmillan.

Jones, Ernest. *Psycho-analysis*. London: Ernest Benn.

——— et al. *Social Aspects of Psycho-analysis*. London: Williams & Norgate.

Isaacs, Susan. *Intellectual Growth in Young Children*. New York: Schocken Books.

———. *Ibid.*, with an Appendix on Children's "Why" Questions by N. Isaacs. London: Routledge & Kegan Paul.

Bridges, K. *The Social and Emotional Development of the Pre-School Child*. London: Routledge & Kegan Paul.

Piaget, Jean. *The Language and Thought of the Child*. London: Routledge & Kegan Paul; New York: Humanities Press.

————. *Judgment and Reasoning in the Child*. London: Routledge & Kegan Paul; New York: Humanities Press.

————. *The Child's Conception of the World*. London: Routledge & Kegan Paul; New York: Humanities Press.

————. *The Child's Conception of Physical Causality*. London: Routledge & Kegan Paul; New York: Humanities Press.

————. *The Moral Judgments of the Young Child*. London: Routledge & Kegan Paul; New York: Free Press.

Stern, W. *The Psychology of Early Childhood*. London: Allen & Unwin.

Stutsman. *Mental Measurement of Pre-School Children*. Cleveland: World.

de Kok, W. *New Babes for Old*. London: Victor Gollancz.

Murchison, Carl (ed.). *Handbook of Child Psychology*. London: Humphrey Milford; New York: Russell & Russell.

Johnson, Harriet M. *Children in the Nursery School*. London: Alllen & Unwin; New York: Fernhill House.

## EDUCATION: THEORY AND PRACTICE

Nunn, Sir T. P. *Education: Its Data and First Principles*. London: Edward Arnold; New York: St. Martin's Press.

Montessori, Maria. *Dr. Montessori's Own Handbook*. London: Heinemann; New York: Schocken Books.

Wells, H. G. *Floor Games*. London: Frank Palmer.

Drummond, M. *The Gateways of Learning*. London:
University of London Press.

Isaacs, Susan. *The Children We Teach*. London: University of London Press.

## BIOLOGY

(*a*) For Parents—

Thomas, J. A., and Geddes, P. *Sex*. London: Home
University Library.

March, N. *Towards Racial Health*. London: Routledge & Kegan Paul.

(*b*) For Little Children—

de Schweinitz, Karl. *How a Baby Is Born*. With
Foreword by Dr. C. W. Kimmins. London:
Routledge & Kegan Paul.

(*c*) For Older Children—

Williams-Ellis, A. *How You Began*. With Preface
by J. B. S. Haldane. London: Gerald Howe.

(*d*) For Adolescents—

Wright, Helena. *What Is Sex?* London: Noel
Douglas.

Stopes, M. *The Human Body*. New York: Putnam.

Parents and nurses would also find great practical
help in dealing with pre-school children, in the weekly
journal *The Nursery World* (London: Ernest Benn).

## PLAYTHINGS AND EDUCATIONAL TOYS

Paul & Marjorie Abbatt, Ltd., supply a variety of
excellent playthings and constructive material for little
children at 94 Wimpole Street, London W.1.

In the U.S., a wide variety of educational toys are available through the Montessori Materials Center, 175 Fifth Avenue, New York City; and Creative Playthings Inc., 1 Rockefeller Plaza, New York City, and Edinburgh Road, Cranbury, N.J.

# INDEX